THE AMERICAN STOCK CAR

WILLIAM BURT

MBI Publishing Company

Acknowledgments

I greatly appreciate the help I received from all the folks at the International Motorsports Hall of Fame in Talladega, Alabama - especially Betty Carlan and Jim Freeman. Much of the research for this book was conducted there and their immense archives and huge collection of significant historical stock cars were both of great benefit. Also, another "thank you" to Michael Rompf, Paul Wise, Nathan Sims and David Pearson for allowing me to ask many, many stupid questions.

First published in 2001 by MBI Publishing Company, Galtier Plaza, Suite 200, 380 Jackson Street, St. Paul, MN 55101-3885 USA

MBI Publishing Company books are also available at discounts in bulk quantity for industrial or sales-promotional use. For details write to Special Sales Manager at Motorbooks International Wholesalers & Distributors, Galtier Plaza, Suite 200, 380 Jackson Street, St. Paul, MN 55101-3885 USA.

Library of Congress Cataloging-in-Publication Data Available

ISBN 0-7603-0977-9

Edited by Peter Bodensteiner
Designed by LeAnn Kuhlmann

Printed in China

On the front cover: Jeff Gordon's Chevrolet Monte Carlo flies by during the 1997 Pennsylvania 500. *Nigel Kinrade*

Buck Baker pilots the very successful, fuel-injected 1957 Chevrolet through the second turn at North Carolina's Asheville-Weaverville Speedway on his way to victory. *Don Hunter*

On the Endpapers: Herb Thomas won seven races in 1951 driving a 1951 Hudson Hornet. Here he drives inside of Fonty Flock. International Motorsports Hall of Fame

On the frontispiece: A mid-1960s Mercury Marauder is being prepared for the track. *International Motorsports Hall of Fame*

On the title page: David Pearson and Richard Petty bring the field around for the start of the 1974 Daytona 500. *Don Hunter*

On the back cover: Because of the left-only turns of oval-track racing, a car's right front tire takes the most abuse. Seen here is the dramatic result of a right-front tire failure. *International Motorsports Hall of Fame*

All the elements of a modern NASCAR effort are evident in this photo: A neatly prepared, aerodynamic race car, sponsorship from a major corporation, and a well-drilled crew ready to rip off a quick pit stop.

On the Contents and Epilogue page: By 1971, the winged cars that had been so popular in recent years had been legislated out of existence, as evidenced by this wingless field of racers. *International Motorsports Hall of Fame*

Contents

Introduction

While putting this book together, my friend Marcus Embry and I were shooting pictures of a few of the stock cars in the International Motorsports Hall of Fame, just outside the Talladega Superspeedway in Alabama. As we pulled each car outside to shoot the pictures, my job was to climb into the car and steer and brake as a tractor pulled it out of the museum. What made this job extraordinarily difficult was the knowledge that, with a flip of the starter switch, most of these cars would crank right up. I suppose there is a bit of larceny in all of us, and I could see myself making my getaway down I-20 in Bobby Allison's Daytona-winning 1988 Buick, or in the K&K Insurance 1969 Dodge Daytona. Hard choice.

The first car we pulled out was a 1962 Catalina. Then we shot Tiny Lund's old Ford Galaxie. Later we graduated to the 1960s and I piloted the aforementioned 1969 Dodge Daytona (at a blistering 1.5 miles per hour). Next was Dale Earnhardt's 1980 Monte Carlo. Toward the end I found myself in Bobby Allison's gold and white Buick. As a great fan and as someone who thinks Bobby was the greatest stock car racer to ever compete, I must rate this car as the greatest I have ever sat in.

It was about this time that my appreciation for the early drivers skyrocketed. In Allison's Buick I felt as though I were in a cocoon. The seat wrapped tightly but comfortably around me. The spiderweb of strong steel roll bars gave me a strong sense of security. It was a pure racing machine. Compared to the cars of the 1960s and 1970s . . . well, there was no comparison. While the earlier cars had some form of

Stock car racing began to catch on in the late 1940s. The war was over and the days of rations and fighting were over. Many young men, and a few women, were looking for excitement, and they found it running the dirt tracks. While the cars have changed dramatically, the action remains the same. Here an early race tangle turns many in the wrong direction. Future greats Buck Baker (Number 7, far right) and Fireball Roberts (Number 11, upper left) were both involved in the accident. Compared to the modern stock car, there were few modifications on the cars in the late 1940s. Engines were massaged and any unnecessary weight was taken off, but the body and suspension were stock.
International Motorsports Hall of Fame

roll cage, it was nowhere as comforting. The seats in the early cars were basically stock and gave about as much support as a school bus seat. The old cars were big, heavy, and had a higher center of gravity. Look under the hood—there's no power steering. It's hard enough to imagine running a modern stock car at 190 miles per hour. It's terrifying to imagine running 160 in the cars of the early 1960s.

The cars have come a long way. They evolved from beat-up, 10-year-old jalopies to stock, off-of-the-showroom-floor racers. Then racers blended stock cars with fabrications and moderate parts interchange. Finally they arrived at custom-built, tubular chassis with mostly hand-built bodies. For many years the production cars produced by the factories dictated what was run on the track. Some times the track dictated what the factories produced.

Drivers and crews, while competing in an incredibly competitive and equally dangerous game, did so with all the furies of the human spirit. They fought, they argued, and they cheated. They also laughed, joked, and helped each other. They did not follow the standard path of birth, school, work, and death. They raced instead. They had little or no security. They spent many long hours in great discomfort

In the 1960s roll bars became more commonplace, but safety features in the cars still had a long way to go. Here Dave Mader crawls away from his car after wrecking with Fred Lorenzen during the 1961 Dixie 400 at Atlanta. *International Motorsports Hall of Fame*

By 1971 the days of dirt tracks were over in NASCAR's elite division. The racers had moved exclusively to paved tracks. The circuit began to offer both the drivers and the fans many different tracks. In 1959 the 2.5-mile Daytona Speedway was opened. A few years later the cars began to run the paved half-mile track at Bristol, at right. *International Motorsports Hall of Fame*

working on cars and hauling cars for a short bit of racing.

But most of the early guys smile when they speak of the discomfort. They seem proud of it. The earlier drivers were able to form bonds of camaraderie that don't come as easily today. Because the sport was not as big, the drivers had more time. They spent that time with each other, not only at the track but also at dinner in a local diner after the race. Today's drivers are far too busy with sponsor commitments, personal appearances, and the other trappings of super-stars. Early drivers could have a few beers and get a little crazy without the fear of losing a sponsor worth $15 million a year.

The evolution of the American stock car closely follows the evolution and growth of NASCAR. The National Association of Stock Car Automobile Racing is the organizing and

As the track surfaces improved, and they became longer, with banked turns, the cars' ability to attain speed outpaced their ability to protect the driver in case of an accident. Roll bars had become mandatory but they were often of questionable construction. The rest of the chassis and body were still stock, as this photo from 1964 demonstrates. *International Motorsports Hall of Fame*

promoting force that has made the sport what it is today. Understanding NASCAR is necessary in order to understand how stock car racing became such a large industry, and the most popular form of racing in America.

NASCAR began sanctioning races in 1949. From the 1950s through part of the 1970s, the race cars run on Sunday were modified production cars—versions of the same cars that could be bought at any dealership. All of the cars run on the circuit today are hand-built race cars. Yet engineering and building a Winston Cup car is somewhat of a paradox.

It can be said that Winston Cup cars are on the cutting edge of yesterday's technology. With a steel chassis, a steel body, pushrod V-8 power, and a solid rear axle, Cup cars are not built on modern technology. Teams do not rely on breakthroughs in materials and systems to increase horsepower and improve handling. The teams must refine existing

technology using experience, trial and error, and open minds. That's not to say that fielding a successful Winston Cup team is not as difficult as fielding an Indy, CART, or Formula One team. It's just a different way of going at it.

Nonetheless, calling a Winston Cup car a "stock" car is like calling a Saturn V rocket a "stock" bottle rocket. From a distance (a good distance) with stock paint, no stickers, regular wheels and tires, and no spoiler (and if you squint your eyes some), they kind of look like the version at the dealership.

While many different teams are building cars, they all must conform to specifications established by NASCAR. It is these specifications that eliminate many of today's exotic materials and designs.

Concepts and systems seen in other racing venues, such as turbochargers, overhead cam configurations, advanced aerodynamics, in-car computer telemetry, and extensive use

By the 1970s the teams were altering the cars' frames and substructures. While Detroit began to remove frames and move to the unibody design, the racers added more steel structure to the cars. This meant both more protection for the driver and stiffer, better-handling race cars. This effort would continue, resulting in the steel tube chassis of modern Winston Cup race cars. *International Motorsports Hall of Fame*

9

to help very much. But when all of these small changes are added up, they may be the difference between winning and being an "also ran." Stock cars have become a product of NASCAR's rule book. Really, they have always been a product of the rule book—it's just that the rule book has gotten much bigger.

In the early years of NASCAR, the cars really were stock. Many had lived a perfectly normal life carrying people to town and back before being turned into a race car. Many served double duty, with the racer driving the car to the track, racing it, and then driving it home, if he (hopefully) kept all the wheels on it.

of exotic materials such as carbon fiber and titanium are not allowed in Winston Cup racing. Again, this forces the teams to rely on improving the engineering of old technology and refining the race setup.

Winston Cup teams make many small changes to the cars and engines that, when looked at alone, may not seem

But as racers looked for speed, they found that the factory's approach to horsepower and handling could be improved upon for racing purposes. It was the birth of the setup, the continuing battle between car parts and physics. Racers

If the car passes all of the templates, it is allowed on the track. But racing is racing and there is no guarantee that the car will fit the template when it comes back.

quickly began to figure out how changes to the car's engine and suspension configuration related to lap times. This was good from the clever car builder's point of view, but from the viewpoint of the racing administration, it was and is a mess.

Bill France, the man who founded NASCAR, knew a few things about auto racing better than anyone else. First, he understood that people come to the track and shell out cash for the excitement. If one guy gets too much of an advantage, the excitement drops. When people stop coming to the track, track revenue drops, purses drop, and before long the whole deal is a mess. The playing field had to be kept level. This meant tight rules—but not so tight that teams had no leeway in looking for speed.

In the first few decades of the sport, the teams worked with cars that were being modified from stock. They still got them from the factories and modified them for racing purposes. As the 1970s progressed, this situation was changing dramatically. By the late 1980s and early 1990s, stock car racing had become a more formal sport of science.

The modern Winston Cup car builder has much more to do than his predecessors, but he also has more people to help in the task. Modern diagnostic equipment has allowed the builders to learn more about what is happening to the race car while it is on the track, and to the engine as it is running. All of this information must be analyzed and understood so that it can be used to make the car faster.

So what do we end up with? Between tighter regulations and ever more sophisticated means of seeking small improvements from well-understood technologies, NASCAR gets a field of competitors that is incredibly balanced. Even with four different makes of automobile and more than 40 cars in every field, things are incredibly tight. The difference between sitting on the pole and not qualifying is often only a fraction of a second. The durability designed into today's stock cars, and the regulations that keep the cars so tightly competitive, mean that a Winston Cup race will feature more cars on the lead lap after 500 miles than in any other form of racing.

Is the sport exactly what Bill France Sr. envisioned? Probably not. The cars aren't stock anymore, but they are possibly the toughest, and the most exciting race cars in the world.

Stock car racing was going on long before NASCAR came along, and it could be a rough affair. The tracks were rough, the cars were rough, and the drivers were rough. There were many different promoters in the old days, and sportsmanship was not always enforced. A fight between cars on the track was often followed by a fight between drivers after the race. *International Motorsports Hall of Fame*

The Early Years

During the early twentieth century, Daytona Beach, Florida, was a favored place for testing the limits of automotive technology, where the pioneers of speed would send their cars screaming down the flat, packed beach as spectators sat on the dunes and cheered. When speeds continued to climb, the serious speed guys went west to the Bonneville Salt Flats' better surface. This was good for the drivers, but it left the people on the dunes with nothing to watch. The last speed runs ended in the mid-1930s, and one of the last spectators was Bill France. France missed the events and soon began to scheme to keep racing alive in Daytona.

It was really an accident that France was in Daytona in the first place. He was heading to South Florida with his family, when he ran out of money in Daytona and had to take a job as a house painter to refill his coffer. He ended up staying in Daytona and, in doing so, forever changed the city.

To understand how the modern stock car came to be, we must also understand Bill France, the man who both created and defined NASCAR.

France probably figured out more about automobile racing than anyone else in the history of America, and as much about promotion as anyone since P. T. Barnum. My only proof of such a bold statement is in the evidence of his labors. It is now impossible to separate NASCAR from the history of the stock car. NASCAR has shaped what stock cars are.

Stock cars did race before NASCAR became a sanctioning body, but the sport was changed tremendously by the vision and the perseverance of "Big Bill" France. He was the driving force who organized and united stock car racing in America. In doing so he gave the South a sport of it own, built a racing empire, and amassed a vast personal fortune.

The ultimate success of stock car racing does not rely on speed, competition, or excitement. These elements have existed in every form of racing since the sport began, from drag racing to road racing, to open wheel racing, and stock car racing. The key to the success of stock car racing has been the ability to sell it. France blueprinted this racing success story almost singlehandedly.

In the 1930s and 1940s, as France was getting his start, racing was far from what it is today. Open-wheel racing had

been the racing flavor of choice in America since the turn of the century. The American Automobile Association (AAA) is generally recognized as the first sanctioning body to sanction races with modifieds, which were versions of cars that were not always stock, but that almost always had fenders. The AAA's first events were in the West and Midwest in the late 1930s.

Within a few years, the modifieds began to run in the South. In the early years of the sport, the modifieds that raced on the track could also be found hauling moonshine on the road. Some of the best at both of these tasks were the

Fords of the late 1930s. They were powered by Ford's flat-head V-8, which had a displacement of 239 cubic inches, was capable of putting out close to 100 horsepower, and would propel the car to speeds over 100 miles per hour. The engine's displacement could be easily increased to 254 cubic inches, but many of these V-8s were bored out to as much as 290 cubic inches.

The car's suspension was good for the times, and the trunk was large enough to haul a good-sized load of whiskey. These cars made many laps skidding and banging on dirt tracks all over the country.

NASCAR's early meetings were a far cry from what they are today. Here Big Bill France (with cap) and company share a small desk in a small room. While NASCAR is currently a megabusiness with great facilities, its beginning was as humble as any new, struggling business. *International Motorsports Hall of Fame*

Right and Below:
France knew that the cost of popularity was promotion. There was little that France would not do to get potential fans' attention. France used everything from a pretty girl to an elephant. The trick was to get attention. He knew that once he got them to the track, many would be hooked. France displayed the NASCAR emblem wherever he could. This year's youth champion could become a stock car champion in 15 years.
International Motorsports Hall of Fame

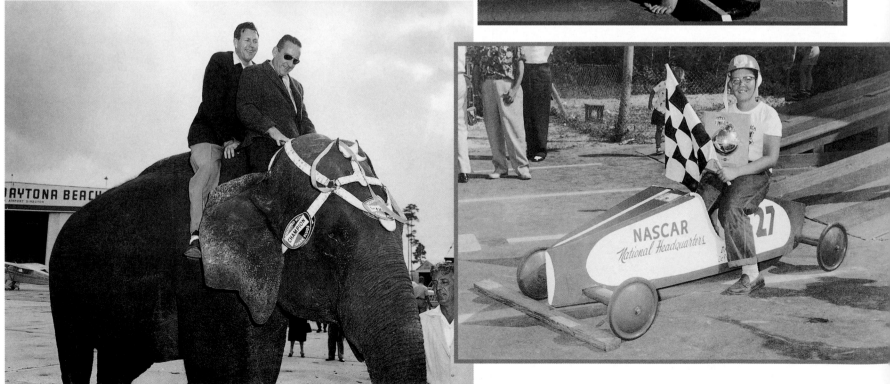

16

So, stock car racing was already rampant before NASCAR was able to lasso it, corral it, and guide it. The problem was that many sanctioning bodies competed with each other, and each one of them produced a champion. This often confused both the public and the press. France understood the problem that this posed for the sport in general. He started NASCAR in hopes of creating one powerful sanctioning body that would attract the best drivers and by providing ample championship money, get them to participate in every race.

Early on, France laid out the mission statement for his new sanctioning body. It read, "The purpose of this association is to unite all stock car racing under one set of rules; to set up a benevolent fund and a national point standings system whereby only one stock car driver will be crowned national champion." It would take years, but France's vision ultimately would be successful.

If you think of France's plan for stock car racing in the shape of a wheel, the racing on the track unquestionably would form the hub. France also built spokes that allowed the sport to reach from this hub deep into mainstream

Above: The old Fords were favorites of the stock car racer. They had good power for the times, an adequate suspension, and a trunk that was large enough to carry a profitable load of moonshine when the driver needed a few extra bucks. *International Motorsports Hall of Fame*

Left: Throughout the twentieth century, the Indianapolis 500 has been the biggest race in America. France saw NASCAR as a method of generating the type of popularity that the Indy 500 enjoyed with stock production vehicles instead of heavily engineered, hand-built race cars. *International Motorsports Hall of Fame*

17

track. Bobby Allison once told me he felt NASCAR was so much more popular than CART or the Indy Racing League because the fan can more easily imagine himself behind the wheel of a stock car than an open-wheel car.

Another of France's spokes was to connect large businesses to racing, in the form of sponsorship. Without steady sponsorship, the only way a car owner can pay to race is with prize money and cash out of his own pocket.

Look, for instance, at the first race at Rockingham in the 2001 season. Steve Park won the race and received $144,593 in prize money. The tire bill alone for such a run is about $21,000 (15 sets at $1,400 a set). That's just for tires. That doesn't include the cost of the car, its engines, the team's employees, research and development, a hauler, a shop, and the other zillion little things needed to run a race car. Nowadays if you see an unsponsored car run for long you know the owner has very deep pockets.

France recognized the high costs of racing early on. In the beginning years of NASCAR, teams had to survive on winnings and promotional bonuses (if you were a big-name driver you might get a little money for just showing up). But overall, the money was very tight. As a result, many drivers ran a limited schedule, running only when they could make money. This often meant that they would not travel very far to race, preventing the sport from growing to a national

With NASCAR's help, the factories learned that racing results would influence what consumers bought. For many years the public could drive the same cars the racers drove. Here Dodge promotes its new Charger Daytona to the public with the race version accompanying it. *International Motorsports Hall of Fame*

America. These spokes were the ultimate reasons for the success and popularity of the sport on a mainstream level.

One spoke allowed fans to relate their own cars to those racing on the track. While other forms of racing were heavily modifying their cars to improve their performance, France wanted to keep the cars as stock as possible. In the early years of NASCAR, the cars were pretty much identical to the cars being driven on the road. In later years they became more and more modified, but they never lost their "stock" tags.

A NASCAR Ford Taurus and a stock Taurus are as different as Secretariat and a plow mule, but they still have the same name and the same general shape. The race car may have a Laughlin chassis and a Roush body and engine, but the car is still called a Ford Taurus. A fan with a Taurus station wagon parked outside the speedway forms a connection to Jack Roush and Mark Martin and the action on the

The budgets of the early racers were low, and the money usually came from the driver. Sponsorship was very limited, but advertising for a local business might generate a few extra bucks. As the sport grew it became harder and harder to run without a sponsor. Now it is virtually impossible. The cost of a couple of sets of tires is now more than an early racer's entire yearly budget. To pay the bills, team owners will plaster decals anywhere they can. Being competitive today requires $8–$10 million. While past sponsorship often trumpeted automotive products, modern cars promote anything from washing powder to cartoons. *International Motorsports Hall of Fame*

level. Further, this meant that fans couldn't count on seeing their favorite driver if they went to a race.

France knew that sponsorship was the honey pot that each level of the racing food chain—drivers, car owners, track owners, and promoters—could eat from. But sponsors would only come if they saw a direct benefit from their advertising. Since the likelihood of such a benefit was tied to the number of people watching the race, it meant that the sport's promotion controlled the primary flow of money into the sport.

Another spoke connected stock car racing to the OEM companies. Detroit would learn that cars that win on Sunday sell on Monday. More important, France believed, manufacturers would use their successes on the track as a promotional tool in their marketing efforts. If a car maker placed an advertisement in the paper bragging on a win, it was not only advertising its car, it was also advertising for NASCAR and stock car racing.

More important to the teams was the fact that if the automobile manufacturers really wanted to win, they would put their weight behind research and development efforts, and they would provide many, many parts to the teams. This mainly helped the "factory" teams (those with a direct working relationship with the factory), but it also helped the other teams. Since the factory teams were constantly getting

free (or very reasonably priced) factory parts, there were plenty of "hand-me-downs" for the other teams.

The final spoke of France's wheel of NASCAR success was to help fans connect to the drivers. To do this, it was very important that the field be consistent from race to race.

By running the same group of drivers every week, France could create a more permanent fan base. Although he arranged to pay appearance fees to some of the more notable drivers, France struggled with this situation for many years before regular drivers consistently ran all of the races.

It took France many years and many battles to build all of these spokes. But, through his guidance and leadership (and later, the guidance and leadership of his son), stock car racing has become the most popular form of automobile racing in the nation.

NASCAR's first official season was set to run in 1948, and there were no superstars. The fledgling sanctioning body had been formed in late 1947 and on February 21, 1948, NASCAR was officially incorporated.

France started his racing organization with three divisions, and to the surprise of many, listed the "Strictly Stock" series as the main attraction. The other classes, Modified

Stocks and Roadsters, ran very different types of cars. These classes ultimately supported the Strictly Stock class much the way that the NASCAR Craftsman Truck Series and the Busch Grand National Series support the Winston Cup Series today. Placing the stock class as the top series was a departure from the norm of the times.

Other sanctioning bodies tended to favor the modified car classes, as the cars were faster, handled better, and thus were deemed more exciting. France, however, figured that the connection between the fans and the sport would grow if the cars on the track were the same as the cars that they drove.

But this plan had problems from the beginning. The Germans and the Japanese get credit for being the first to screw up France's agenda: Because of America's recent involvement in World War II, no new cars were built for consumer use during the war years, and the automakers were having trouble building enough cars to satisfy postwar demand. As a result, most fans were still driving 10-year-old cars in 1948. Watching a driver beat up a brand-new car at

One would think that a uniform paved surface would give the racers more control. But this was often not the case. This race took place on the McCormick Field Speedway in Asheville, North Carolina. *International Motorsports Hall of Fame*

the track tended to leave a bad taste in fans' mouths, and France knew it.

Because of this situation, and the lack of success with the Roadster class, he had to rely on the Modified Stock class to keep his young association alive in 1948. France did not want the modifieds to be his big draw, but he needed them to keep his show alive for the time being.

This type of thinking would always characterize France. He held on to his visions like a bulldog, but if he had to depart from his plan temporarily to make progress, he would. Then he would wait patiently for the circumstances to change so that he could proceed with his big plans.

There were 52 modified races in the 1948 NASCAR season. About the only similarity to the modern Winston Cup season was that the season started in Daytona and ended in Georgia (Columbus, not Atlanta). The total prize money for all of the races that season was a little over $100,000. The total championship purse for the year was

Early suspensions left much to be desired. Stock parts were all the racers had to work with, and the result was often more horsepower than handling. Weak springs on the right side and a high center of gravity put this racer up on two wheels. *International Motorsports Hall of Fame*

$5,000, to be split between the top 20 drivers. The championship paid $1,250 and was eventually won by Red Byron.

1949

Nineteen forty-nine turned out to be a big year for stock car racing, and a big year for France's Strictly Stock Division. Although it was not successful in 1948, France wanted to revive the stock class, as he had a great deal of faith in its ultimate success. Meanwhile, the automakers were catching up with production and more new cars were becoming available. Also, France had noticed that other sanctioning bodies were passing over strictly stock cars in favor of modified stock cars.

Competition was stiff among NASCAR and other sanctioning bodies, like the National Stock Car Racing Association (NSCRA), the United Stock Car Racing Association (USCRA), the National Auto Racing League (NARL), and the American Stock Car Racing Association (ASCRA), all of which were trying to steal some thunder from the open-wheel races of the time.

Each organization was eyeing the others, looking for an advantage. The rivalry was especially fierce between France's NASCAR and Olin Bruton Smith's NSCRA. They competed in the same geographic area and were trying to attract the same fans and the same drivers.

In February 1949, France took a shot at his Strictly Stock class with an experimental Strictly Stock event run in Florida at the Broward Speedway before a roadster race. Bob Flock won the 10-mile, five-lap event, but it was hard to gauge the effect on the fans.

France's next attempt at the Strictly Stocks was a bolder affair. On June 19, 1949, France staged a 150-mile (now considered a short race, but a very long distance for the time) Strictly Stock race with $5,000 in purse money.

This race caught fans, drivers, and competing sanctioning bodies off guard. Because most drivers were competing in modifieds and roadsters, some wondered if France would be able to attract a complete field. Once again France looked to the obvious. Since almost anyone with a stock production car could enter, he knew at least 33 people would show up ready to race. He was right.

The race took place in Charlotte, on a 3/4-mile dirt track cut into the North Carolina countryside. Unlike his first attempt, this time France would be better able to gauge the effect on the crowd. The front gates, scheduled to open at noon, had to be opened early because of the huge traffic

jam coming into the track. (France would always try to accommodate the customer.) Though some estimates were higher, France later said that around 13,000 people paid to watch the race.

The size of the crowd gave France a huge boost of confidence. All along he wanted the Strictly Stock Division to stand on its own, and after this race it appeared as though it could. The field of 33 cars ranged from 1946 models to 1949 models, 14 of which made the start.

Nine manufacturers were represented, including Lincolns, Hudsons, Oldsmobiles, Fords, Buicks, Chryslers, a Mercury, a Cadillac, and even a Kaiser. Bob Flock, a racer who would tally four wins in his career, won the pole position in a 1946 Hudson.

Engine overheating was a problem for a number of teams during the race. The cooling systems of the day may have been adequate for low-speed road driving, but they were not yet up to the rigors of high-speed racing. Bob Flock was sidelined with engine problems, but he would reenter the race as a relief driver for Sara Christian.

In the race's only accident, Lee Petty went tumbling in his 1946 Buick Roadmaster in turn three. Apparently he was racing the car without permission—it is said that after the accident he sat by the track wondering how to tell his wife what he did to the car.

As the laps wore down, Glenn Dunnaway and his 1947 Ford had the field covered. The nearest challenger, a 1949 Lincoln driven by Jim Roper, was overheating, so Roper was forced to

Crowds varied from event to event, but they always got a show. Anyone who had a car could race, and the result was often a kind of amateur racer stew in the first few turns.
International Motorsports Hall of Fame

slow down to nurse his ride to a second-place finish.
Dunnaway took the checkered flag after 197 laps with a
three-lap lead.

After the race, Al Crisler, NASCAR's first technical
inspector, got a quick initiation into his job. When inspecting Dunnaway's car after the race it was discovered that the
rear springs of the Ford had been altered. This violated the
"strictly stock" rules of the division and the win was taken
from Dunnaway and given to Roper.

At the time few knew that what would become the most
successful stock car racing organization ever had put its first
big success under its belt. Fewer yet could imagine the great
similarities between this race and those that would take
place 50 years later with dramatically different cars.

The season's second race took place on the 4.15-mile
Beach & Road Course in Daytona Beach, Florida. If you
think today's crew chiefs have a hard time figuring out
setups for specific tracks, imagine coming up with one for
this place. Each circuit took the drivers down the beach,
through a turn that put them onto an access road running
parallel to the beach, and finally to a turn that would return
them to the beach. As the cars made their way around the
course, the surface of the sandy track changed continually.
Twenty-eight drivers qualified to compete in the 40-lap,
166-mile event. Three women—Louise Smith, Ethel Flock
Mobley, and Sara Christian—qualified and started the race.

There would only be six more Strictly Stock races in
1949. The rest were run on dirt tracks ranging from 1/2 mile

Sara Christian gets ready to go racing. In the first few years of NASCAR, women drivers were quite common. Ethel Flock Mobley, Louise Smith, Mildred Williams, and Ruth Nixon all drove races in 1949. *International Motorsports Hall of Fame*

Below: Curtis Turner (Number 41), prepares to pass the Number 32 of Bill Haddock. Curtis drove his Oldsmobile to win the 1949 Strictly Stock Division. Bill France's sanctioning body had a season under its belt and would ultimately be incredibly successful. Fifty years later, however, his "strictly stock" cars had evolved into heavily engineered, hand-built race cars. *International Motorsports Hall of Fame*

to 1 mile in length. There were two more races in North Carolina, two in Pennsylvania, one in Virginia, and one in New York. Another point of interest in the 1949 season was the relatively large number of women drivers. Ethel Flock Mobley, (sister of Fonty, Bob, and Tim Flock), Sara Christian, Mildred Williams, Louise Smith, and Ruth Nixon all raced in 1949.

When the 1949 season ended, Red Bryon was crowned champion with six starts, two wins, four top-5 finshes, and four top-10 finshes. His total winnings for the year were $5,800.

In the first year of competition, Oldsmobiles ruled the track. They won five of the eight races, with Red Byron and Bob Flock driving Oldsmobiles to two wins apiece, and Curtis Turner winning once. Lincoln won twice and Lee Petty won one race for Plymouth, after switching from the Buick he wrecked.

The foundation for the sport had been laid. During the next decade it would move from the creation stage to the survival stage.

Although the sport was in its infancy, heading into the 1950s it was unmistakably exciting. During the 1950s NASCAR would extend its roots into the sports culture of America and become a polished, professional entity. *International Motorsports Hall of Fame*

Chapter Two

The 1950s

The best seed for stock car racing, NASCAR, had been planted in the late 1940s by Big Bill France. The 1950s would be the decade in which the roots would either take hold or wither, like so many other racing associations. The keys to success would be better attendance, more sponsorship, and increased awareness—making the sport known to all, so that new fans could be secured. In order to do this, the sport would need more promotion from NASCAR, track owners, the auto manufacturers, and the sponsors. NASCAR would also rely on the great action on the track and the top drivers. They would become the stars who would lead fans to create bonds that would emotionally (and financially) link them to the sport.

The fledgling association would rely on a sometimes tenuous alliance of the NASCAR administration, the drivers and teams, the track owners, the sponsors, and the manufacturers. It would prove successful, but there would be fender banging in the offices as well as on the track.

After the short but successful 1949 season, NASCAR kept the momentum going. In 1950 the Strictly Stock Division schedule grew from 8 to 19 races. France, always the promoter, also changed the name of his premier series. The technical, nonemotional name Strictly Stock was dropped in favor of the tag "Grand National." France picked up this name from horse racing, feeling it was much more dynamic and would better capture the interest of fans. It was yet another example of France's superior marketing skills. In 1950 the series continued to run races on dirt tracks from New York to Florida, and as far west as Ohio and Indiana.

Competition from rival series once again shaped France's plans. The CSRA (Central States Racing Association), another stock car series, was planning the country's first 500-mile stock car race. The idea of a race of such incredible length had caught the imagination of both the fans and the press. As one might imagine, this fascination didn't escape Bill France's attention either.

This 500-mile dream was obviously influenced by the nation's biggest racing event, the Indianapolis 500. For stock car racing to be taken seriously, and for it to reach its potential, many felt it was critical to race this distance.

The track that would host the first 500-mile stock car race owed its existence to the Indy 500 and a peanut farmer named Harold Brasington.

Brasington had attended the Indianapolis 500, and as early as 1933, he had dreamed of stock cars running 500 miles on a paved track. The only problem was that there was no paved track suitable for the race. So Brasington began talking about building one in the small town of Darlington, South Carolina. Everyone thought he was crazy, but in 1949 he built his long-imagined track on a piece of land that had been home only to peanuts and cotton.

The result of Brasington's effort was the Darlington International Raceway, a place that is still revered in stock

Darlington was the first paved track built specifically for stock car racing. Its unique egg-shaped design owes itself to an effort to save the landowner's minnow pond. With its wide turns at one end and its narrow turns at the other, the track has always been a challenge to both driver and crew chief. It is a track worthy of the motto, "Too tough to tame." *International Motorsports Hall of Fame*

car circles. A 1.25-mile speedway with banked turns, Darlington was the blueprint for the tracks of the future. Brasington wanted the track to be a true oval, but stock car fans know the track wound up with a unique egg-shaped layout that makes car setup a headache for drivers and crew chiefs to this day. The turns at one end of the track had to be narrowed to allow the landowner to keep a minnow pond located on the track site.

France was nervous about staging a 500-mile race. He feared the stock race cars of the Grand National Division might suffer too many mechanical problems if they raced such a long distance. If most of the cars broke, his premier series might become a laughingstock. But the CSRA was pushing the issue, considering the treacherous dirt oval of Lakewood Speedway near Atlanta, or the new Darlington Speedway for their 500.

France realized that if a 500-mile race was going to happen, he had better be a part of it. When he heard that the CSRA was having difficulties getting enough drivers, France once again adapted to circumstance and offered a deal.

The first 500-mile stock car race would be cosanctioned by NASCAR and the CSRA. The idea of running the race

Early fields were open to whoever showed up, and for the big races many showed up. The first race at Darlington featured more than 70 cars. *International Motorsports Hall of Fame*

While his performance on the track was good enough to win a championship in 1950, Lee Petty (along with Red Byron) was taken out of contention when he was penalized for racing in non-NASCAR sanctioned races. *International Motorsports Hall of Fame*

29

The Oldsmobile Rocket 88 was the hot ride in the early 1950s. Here Numbers 69 and 14 weave their way through the field. The 3,600-pound cars had either a 247-cubic-inch or 303-cubic-inch V-8 that put out 130 to 140 horsepower. Today's cars weigh 3,400 pounds and have close to 800 horsepower. *International Motorsports Hall of Fame*

to the upstart NASCAR. Nash Motor Company was the first automaker to officially "hook up" with NASCAR in both a competitive and a promotional manner. It offered contingency money, backed some cars (the first factory-backed effort), and presented a new car to the 1950 champion. Nash had only one win (a 1951 victory at Charlotte with Curtis Turner at the wheel) before exiting the sport, but France welcomed its relationship with NASCAR.

During the season, the championship points lead changed 10 times. In all, seven drivers led at some point. Curtis Turner won four events driving his Oldsmobile. Dick Linder won three times in an Olds. No other driver won more than one race. Bill Rexford, also in one of the big, powerful Oldsmobiles, won only one race, but consistency (and not being penalized like Petty and Byron) won him the championship by 110.5 points. He was only 23 years old and remains the series' youngest champion.

Without a doubt, in 1950 the Oldsmobile Rocket 88 was the car to beat. It was the only winning product for General Motors, but win it did. In 1949 the car was powered by a 247-cubic-inch V-8 engine. The engine's displacement was later increased to 303 cubic inches, and it was rated at 130 to 140 horsepower. That's not considered much now, but at the time it was plenty to power the 3,600-pound car to victory.

The Oldsmobiles were so popular with drivers that in the early 1950s, they often made up half of the field. Oldsmobiles won 10 of the season's 19 races. The other 9 wins were split between Plymouth (4 wins), Mercury (2 wins), and Lincoln (2 wins). Ford won its first Grand National event in 1950 at the Dayton Speedway, a half-mile dirt track in Dayton, Ohio. Jimmy Florian drove the car, a 1950 model.

1951

NASCAR's third year was marked by a flurry of activity. Drivers were suspended, a new sponsorship deal was inked, the sport moved west, and there was even a battle with the government. The season exploded from 19 races in 1950 to 41 races for 1951. Herb Thomas won seven times in his Oldsmobile on his way to the championship. Thomas only raced in 34 of the 41 races and did not win a race in 1951 until the 16th race of the year, a 100-mile event on a half-mile dirt track in Heidelberg, Pennsylvania.

Running a partial schedule was common in the early years of the sport. In fact, Buddy Sherman finished sixth in the 1951 championship with only seven starts, showing just how far France had yet to go to produce consistent fields. However, racers were still operating on shoestring budgets and often could not afford to run every event.

In order to make more prize money available to the drivers, France had to generate more revenue. There were

on dirt was abandoned, and it was scheduled for Darlington on September 4, 1950. It was called the "Southern 500," and it is still run every Labor Day weekend. NASCAR's drivers and crews consider it to be one of their most prestigious races.

France fulfilled his pledge to bring drivers to the event, filling the field with 75 (yes, 75) cars. The crowd was estimated at around 25,000 fans. More than $25,000 was offered in prize money, the most ever for a stock car event.

Johnny Mantz took top honors, winning this first race at Darlington. He drove a Westmoreland/France 1950 Plymouth and finished an incredible nine laps ahead of second-place finisher Fireball Roberts, who drove a 1950 Oldsmobile.

France was beginning to stack up successes, but it was still difficult to keep drivers committed to NASCAR. He turned to a time-honored solution: punishment. Drivers running for championship money could be heavily penalized for a lack of commitment to NASCAR, and could lose all accumulated championship points for racing in non-NASCAR sanctioned events. In 1950 it happened to Red Byron twice and Lee Petty once, and it cost both of them dearly.

Many sanctioning bodies still claimed a piece of stock car racing, but one manufacturer decided to pay extra attention

two major ways to do this. The first was at the gate. More fans paying to watch a race meant more track revenue and a bigger purse. The other way to raise revenue was to increase the role of sponsorship. This meant finding companies that would pay to have their name associated with stock car racing. In 1951 France made moves in both of these areas.

France tried to expand the fan base of his association to the western United States, setting up six races far west of the sport's mostly southern tracks. When he staged a race in Gardena, California, on a half-mile dirt track, his association could finally be considered "coast to coast."

A move by France to attract more fans was to have Bill Holland run some Grand National events. Holland had

raced very successfully at Indianapolis, the country's biggest and most publicized American racing event at the time. He finished second in 1947 as a rookie, second in 1948, and won the event in 1949.

In what has to be considered one of the stupidest moves ever by a racing association, the AAA, which sanctioned the

It wasn't just Ford, GM, and Chrysler products that raced in NASCAR in the early 1950s. A few others were Nash, Studebaker, Kaiser, Hudson, and even Jaguar. Above, a big Packard barrels down the track. At left, Joie Ray prepares to compete in his Henry J. The Henry J was relatively light and was also a favorite of drag racers. *International Motorsports Hall of Fame*

Indianapolis race, suspended Holland for the entire 1951 season for racing in a three-lap Lion's Club charity race. When France heard about this, he made a beeline to Holland to suggest that he go stock car racing with NASCAR. This would immediately give NASCAR a nationally known, big-name driver competing on the circuit. Although he wasn't very successful, with one top-five in seven starts, Holland's presence did increase the interest of both the press and the public in NASCAR.

Another public relations success in 1951 was the Motor City 250. Detroit was celebrating its 250th birthday, and France suggested a race featuring all of the makes of cars built in Detroit at the Michigan State Fairgrounds, which had a 1-mile dirt track.

At this time, most of the manufacturers did not have an interest in NASCAR, as they do today. But Detroit liked the idea, and on August 12 they dropped the green flag. Sixteen different brands raced, including all of the major brands, plus Packard, Nash, Hudson, Studebaker, and even a Henry J. Tommy Thompson won the race in a 1951 Chrysler.

The race was a pivotal success for France. Not only was there great fan interest (more than 16,000 paid to watch), but a great deal of interest was generated among the automotive leaders of Detroit, many of whom were on hand to watch the event.

Incidentally, the toughness of the stock cars of the time was demonstrated in full when Lee Petty again tumbled down the track, rolling his 1951 Plymouth. Incredibly, Petty went on to finish 13th in the race, a tribute to the great strength of the car's factory body.

All of these events helped increase the sport's fan base. But France also wanted to hook up with some large, well-respected companies for sponsorship deals. In 1951 he completed the series' first big sponsorship arrangement with the Pure Oil Company, which agreed to become NASCAR's official fuel supplier. This relationship was a prelude to things to come.

NASCAR fans have become so accustomed to sponsor colors on every race car that it is hard to imagine stock car racing any other way. But during the sport's early years, the cars could be quite bland visually. That's not to say the racing was not exiting—it was. But there was not much glitter. The cars were mostly black with a number on the door, and that was usually hastily hand-painted.

Another challenge for France in 1951 came from an entirely different direction. Legislation was proposed to Congress by representatives from California, New Jersey, and North Carolina to ban all forms of automobile racing. Many felt that the combination of speed and automobiles in any form was a detriment. France helped lobby against the bill and it never made it to the floor of Congress.

One of the first moves away from the "strictly stock" ideal occurred in 1951. Stock cars had problems running on rough dirt tracks for long distances, primarily from over-heating and broken suspension parts. Hudson began to provide cars and parts to teams in one of the first examples of true factory support. One of its ideas was to offer some "high performance" parts and list them in its parts catalog as a "severe usage" kit. Doing this made the parts legal under NASCAR rules, as any consumer could purchase the parts from the dealer. In another change, NASCAR allowed teams to install "floating" axles taken from Ford trucks. Stock axles were more likely to break, often causing the cars to flip.

Another change by NASCAR was the rule that Grand National cars would no longer race on tracks shorter than a half-mile. France started the NASCAR Short Track Division to run on these smaller tracks. He also introduced the Sportsman's Division, which was aimed at the weekend racer. This series eventually evolved into today's NASCAR Busch Grand National Series.

The year 1951 also saw the first NASCAR race run under lights, on a half-mile dirt track in Columbia, South Carolina. But the big race in South Carolina was still the Southern 500 at Darlington. In 1951 the largest starting field in NASCAR Winston Cup history (82 cars) raced in the Southern 500.

Oldsmobile continued its domination in 1951. Oldsmobile won 21 races, more than half of the 41 races held that year. Ford and Lincoln were shut out, but Mercury did manage 2 wins late in the season. Chrysler also got its first win when Tommy Thompson won the Detroit 250, the 20th race of the season. But the big story in 1951 was the arrival of Hudson, offering a strong combination of power and handling and taking 12 races in its first season.

For NASCAR racers in the 1950s, having a competitive ride was a matter of choosing the right car, not of building a race car. Because of the strictly stock philosophy, racers had very little leeway in what they could do to the cars and remain legal. As a result, brand loyalty only lasted as long as that brand was competitive. If another model offered a competitive edge, the racers were likely to jump on board. In 1951 they began jumping on the Hudsons. This ride-hopping also resulted in a Nash getting a single win and Studebaker winning three times in 1951.

The 1951 Hudson Hornet was a breed apart. First, it had a relatively aerodynamic body for the times. The car was still powered by a very basic motor—a valve-in-block, 308-cubic-inch, inline six-cylinder. But Hudson offered performance parts, like a dual-carburetor setup, special wheels, shocks, and rear axles.

All these parts came from the factory with real part numbers so they would be considered legal in the eyes of NASCAR. Hudson also dropped the running boards from the car and "dropped" the entire passenger compartment between the frame rails. Hudson ultimately would win 70 Grand National races and three championships. Drivers Herb Thomas and Marshall Teague racked up the most wins in Hudsons. Dick Rathmann, Tim Flock, and Frank Mundy also enjoyed success behind a Hudson's wheel.

1952

One of France's moves in 1952 showed some uncertainty as to the direction NASCAR was to take. Among the sanctioning bodies of the time, the heavyweight was the AAA. It sanctioned all types of racing and, with its control of the Indianapolis 500, was a very formidable foe to

Hudsons had been raced for a while, but in 1951 they began to come on strong. The Hudson offered racers both power and handling. The motor was more than adequate, and Hudson "dropped" the body more between the frame rails, which did wonders for the car's handling by lowering the car's center of gravity. Hudson became the dominator in the early 1950s. Racers of the time couldn't do much in the way of modifications, so choosing the best-handling, most powerful model offered by the manufacturers was critical. Herb Thomas chose well, as he won the 1951 Grand National Championship in his "Fabulous Hudson." Herb Thomas started the 1951 season in a 1950 Plymouth, but by the end of the year he had switched to a 1951 Hudson Hornet. Thomas chalked up seven wins in 34 starts. *International Motorsports Hall of Fame*

Tim Flock drives his Hudson on his way to winning a championship. The Hudson took over from Oldsmobile as the prime ride for 1952. Hudsons won 12 of 41 races in 1951 and 27 of 34 in 1952, a whopping 79 percent. *International Motorsports Hall of Fame*

NASCAR and the other racing organizations of the day. France dreamed of tapping into the atmosphere that drew more than a quarter-million fans through the turnstiles to watch the Indianapolis 500.

So in 1952, France took a stab at open-wheel racing. While they looked much like Indy cars, his "Speedway Division" cars used stock powerplants in hopes that the lower cost would attract new teams. Buck Baker won the first Speedway Division event at Darlington, driving a Cadillac-powered car.

The Speedway Division was a rare case of divergence for France. He knew, however, that if you don't have your hook in the water, you don't catch any fish, so France was always looking for new markets. NASCAR, as an association, was a flexible tool for such exploration. The danger lay in the fact that an effort to promote a new series could cause an existing, successful series to be neglected. Fortunately,

At the half-mile dirt track at the Wilson County Speedway in Wilson, North Carolina, on September 30, 1952, Herb Thomas's Hudson sits on the pole with the 1951 Ford of Bill Snowden (No. 16) starting second. Bob Flock (No. 7) starts fourth in a 1951 Oldsmobile 88. Fonty Flock would win the 100-mile race in his 1952 Olds 88. *International Motorsports Hall of Fame*

France not only knew how to cast, he also knew when to cut bait. The Speedway Division never took off. After seven races were run, Buck Baker was declared the series' one and only champion.

The Grand National season dropped from 41 to 34 races for the 1952 season. The far west races were dropped in 1952, but the series still ranged from Florida up to Pennsylvania and New York. Tim Flock won the championship by 106 points driving a Hudson. Herb Thomas finished second in the points, narrowly missing a second consecutive championship. Earlier in his career he had driven both Oldsmobiles and Plymouths, but he left them at home and started bringing a Hudson to the track. Both Flock and Thomas ended the season with 8 wins.

Oldsmobile dropped from 21 victories in 1951 to 3 in 1952, with Fonty Flock winning 2 of those. Chrysler won 1 race under the command of driver Gober Sosobee. Lee Petty stayed with Plymouth and won 3 times. When the dust settled, Hudson had 27 wins, a manufacturers championship, and a big edge on the competition.

Two major technical advancements made their appearance 1952, including the first documented use of a two-way radio. Driver Al Stevens operated a radio-dispatched tow service for a living and naturally decided to use a two-way radio to communicate with team owner Cotton Bennett and his two spotters during a modified race on February 9, 1952. He finished third in his class, and a new NASCAR mainstay was born. Also, NASCAR mandated the use of roll bars in 1952. Previously, the car's stock body was all the protection the driver had. However, it would be many years before all the roll bars would have adequate structural integrity.

The sponsorship side of France's business also continued to grow. Pure Oil continued its involvement, while other automotive supply companies, such as Champion Spark Plugs, Wynn's, and Miracle Power, put money into the points fund. The Pure Oil Company also gets credit for offering the first racing tire. Until its product arrived, the racers' only option was to use street tires, which often failed.

France wanted the points fund to pay more so that drivers would compete in all of the events. While 1952 champion Tim Flock competed in 33 of the 34 races, not many other drivers could compete that often. For example, sixth place finisher Bill Blair competed in only 19 events. France was still far from delivering a consistent field every week.

1953

In 1953, for the first time, a driver competed in all of the races. Herb Thomas was the only driver to run all 37 races, and it helped him win his second Grand National Championship. Thomas, still driving his Hudson, scored 12 victories along the way. Lee Petty, still a Mopar man but

now in a Dodge, finished second in the championship, scoring 5 wins in 36 starts.

NASCAR also saw some tough times in 1953, particularly in the area of safety. The production cars of the era featured lap-only seat belts and did not have such modern features as shoulder harnesses, collapsible steering wheels, and airbags. The racing speeds overwhelmed the safety features of the Grand National cars, which had little more than stock safety measures protecting the drivers.

On June 20 at Langhorne Speedway in Langhorne, Pennsylvania, part-time driver and car owner Frank Arford was killed when he was thrown from his Oldsmobile during a qualifying crash. The seat brackets had broken during the crash and Arford slipped under the seat belt.

This crash prompted NASCAR to issue a notice urging competitors to reinforce the seats when installing roll bars so that they would not break loose in a crash. Fireball Roberts, who had survived a similar crash in a modified, backed up NASCAR's safety notice.

The seed for the modern roll cage had been planted. Despite such horrific crashes, it would take a while for quality

The Pure Oil Company was one of the first large corporations to see the benefit of a relationship with NASCAR. Fifty years later the list of sponsors in the sport reads like a who's who of American business. Without the sponsors' cash the cars would never have evolved from stock to pure race car. It's sponsorship that allows grown men and women to make a living at the race track. *International Motorsports Hall of Fame*

roll cages to arrive. Early roll bar materials included old plumbing pipe and sometimes even wood 2x4s. But with the addition of roll bars and harnesses, parts that were either fabricated by the team or purchased from a non-OEM supplier, the strictly stock Grand National cars began the migration toward the custom-built, pure race car we see today.

It was not only big issues that were giving France problems. One smaller difficulty centered around the entry forms that NASCAR required racers to fill out and turn in to NASCAR before the race. The racers of the day were not all that good with paperwork. Usually they just showed up at the track, ready to race.

This put NASCAR in a difficult position. France needed drivers and wanted every starting grid at every race

full. On the other hand, NASCAR needed to know how many competitors to expect and who they would be. This information was needed to organize and promote the race. NASCAR tried to make the drivers understand that better promotion meant more prize money, but drivers marched to the beat of their own drums. In the drivers' defense, a lack of funds could keep them from knowing exactly when they could race.

But in 1953 NASCAR created a new rule stating that no points would be awarded to a driver who did not fill out an entry blank. It was a rule that some learned the hard way. More than one driver received no points after a good finish. Eventually, the drivers began to comply. While this issue may sound like a small administrative matter, the creation of this rule was big moment for the sport. France always wanted better organization and driver commitment, and the entry forms helped improve both areas.

A few other interesting events occurred during the 1953 season. One of them took place at Hickory, North Carolina, on August 29. Future 50 race winner and two-time Winston Cup Champion Ned Jarrett competed in his first Grand National race. He finished 11th out of 12 starters on the half-mile dirt track in his 1950 Ford. Another pivotal event was the International Stock Car Grand Prix, held at Langhorne Speedway on June 21. France, always the promoter, put together this unique 200-mile event that was open to both foreign and domestic hardtop automobiles. In his own words, France said, "This NASCAR-sanctioned show is calculated to settle arguments galore about the merits of such imports as Mercedes and Jaguars on a circular track."

Seven American automobile manufacturers were represented and four foreign makes—Porsche, Jaguar, Aston

Above and left: Driver safety became more of a problem as speeds began to grow. Teams thought about horsepower more than safety, and the results began to show. NASCAR stepped in and began the ongoing process of mandating safety features on the cars. The factories also began to learn from racing and experimented with new and radical ideas, such as safety belts. *International Motorsports Hall of Fame*

At The Track

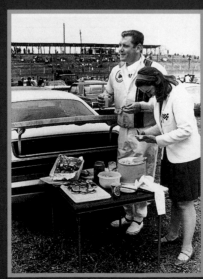

By the 1960s, things were getting better at some facilities. Newer tracks like Daytona gave drivers and crew better accommodations and more room to work. But the song remained the same. Then and now, the garage was filled with men crawling all over and under the car, getting it ready to race. *International Motorsports Hall of Fame*

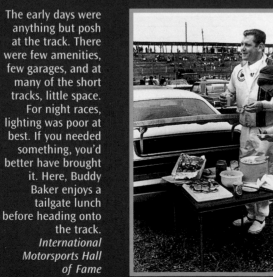

The early days were anything but posh at the track. There were few amenities, few garages, and at many of the short tracks, little space. For night races, lighting was poor at best. If you needed something, you'd better have brought it. Here, Buddy Baker enjoys a tailgate lunch before heading onto the track. *International Motorsports Hall of Fame*

During the 1950s and 1960s, seasons often consisted of 50 or more races, but as the sport grew the schedule became shorter. However, races were usually only one-day affairs. After the modern schedule of 30 or so races started, the individual races became more and more extended. Now a race consumes Friday and the entire weekend.

The teams arrive in the town of the race on Thursday and will be at the track early Friday morning. The first order of business Friday is unloading the gear, setting up the stall in the garage area, and getting the car ready for qualifying. Most teams arrive at the track with a dedicated qualifying engine in the car and ready to go. Qualifying engines are set up a little more on the edge than the race engines. After all, they only have to last a few laps, while the race engine must last 500 miles. During morning practice, teams try to "dial in" the suspension setup.

The first setup tried will most likely be based on previous experience at the track being raced. All previous setups are re-corded and evaluated. A team may start with the same set-up that worked well with at a previous race under basically the same track and weather conditions. As qualifying practice starts, lap times are tracked and the driver's observations about how the car is behaving are also discussed.

Qualifying practice usually consists of two-lap runs, after which the car goes back to the garage for adjustments. Teams may change tire combinations, tire pressures, spring rates, shock settings, wedge adjustments, sway bar combinations, spoiler angles, and even rear-end gear ratios.

In past years, many "qualifying only" parts were put on the cars. Until recently a different, dedicated qualifying radiator was used. Now the rules require that a car must race with the radiator that it qualifies with, eliminating "qualifying radiators" that cannot not properly cool the engine for 500 miles. Once the team feels that the car is running competitively enough to qualify, the practicing stops and the wait for qualifying begins.

Once qualifying is completed, teams shift gears and begin to set up the car for the race. The qualifying engine is taken out of the car and replaced with the race engine. After the motor is swapped, teams change from the qualifying setup to the race setup. The race suspension must be fast and must also be comfortable for the driver for 500 miles. Teams work quickly and usually have the car ready within an hour.

While qualifying practice runs are one or two laps long, the race practice runs are longer. A qualifying setup must be fast as possible as quickly as possible since a qualifying run is only two laps long—a setup that becomes fast after eight laps does not help. However, a race setup must remain fast over long runs. A setup that is fast for two laps and then fades may qualify well, but it won't do much for you in the race.

Over long runs during the race, the car changes. Tires progressively lose their grip the longer they are run. As each

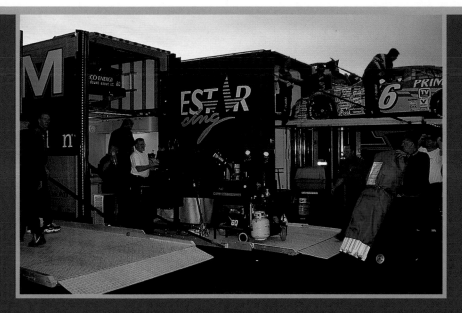

In recent years carts have begun to incorporate video equipment to record pit stops (the camera is extended over the pit area on a lightweight boom), and even small satellite dishes, enabling teams to monitor the television broadcast of the race.

While the stall is being readied, other crew members are still preparing the car. It is not uncommon to find many of the cars in varying states of repair. As the teams finish this preparation, the garage stall is emptied and the team moves to pit road. The cars are pushed to their position on the starting grid, where the driver will take over the racing effort.

The teams' job got a lot easier when they started using transporters. Modern rigs allow the team to carry two cars, five engines, extra transmissions and rear gears, and a ton of suspension parts. The rig will also haul all of the tools that the team needs to work on the car.

gallon of fuel is used, around 6 pounds of weight disappears from the fuel cell. Twenty gallons means around 120 pounds, which can make quite a difference in the handling.

Once all of these setup changes have been made, the cars go back out and practice, recording lap speeds and adjusting the engine and suspension.

The most critical practice session comes after the Saturday main event. For one hour, Winston Cup cars are allowed to practice, doing their final tuning and setup preparation. Known as Happy Hour, this is the last time cars are allowed to practice before the Sunday race. Any car that is wrecked beyond repair during this practice session may be replaced with a back-up car, but the car forfeits the starting position it earned during qualifying and must start the race at the rear of the field.

On Sunday morning, teams begin to set up the pit stall. First the cart is pushed to the pit stall. The cart contains tools, parts, and the tanks that provide the air for the air wrenches used while pitting.

While early racers had to rely on their old Sears and Roebuck tool box, the modern team has a huge, custom, roll-around toolbox. They hold hundreds of pounds of tools—everything needed to work on the car.

The garages at the track are empty on Thursday night, but early Friday morning they are filled with the cars, tools, parts, and crew from 40-plus teams. With the load each team brings in on its transporter, team members will have everything they need throughout the race weekend.

Martin, and Volkswagen—made the field. Although Lloyd Shaw's Jaguar won pole position, Dick Rathmann's Hudson led every lap as domestic cars swept the top five positions. Another paved speedway was available in 1953 in Raleigh, North Carolina, and NASCAR ran a 300-miler on May 30.

Hudson again dominated in 1953, winning 22 of 37 events. Oldsmobile bounced back with 9 wins. Dodge won the rest of the races, led by Lee Petty with an impressive 5 wins. Lincoln had joined Hudson in offering "severe usage" kits during 1953, but the marque failed to find victory lane.

1954

During the 1954 season, the fact that the rule book was thin became more and more apparent. Early stock car racing could be a rough affair. At many races the rules, if there were any, were not always equally enforced. One of NASCAR's stated goals was consistent adherence to the rules, but the young association's success was dependent upon a delicate balance between the top teams, the tracks, and NASCAR.

At times, NASCAR made decisions that were designed more to win the war than the battle. Some competitors were treated as if the rules did not affect them. But as the series gained momentum, the discretionary decisions that helped keep the important players happy could ultimately hurt the sport's integrity.

France decided to clamp down and adhere more strictly to policy. In 1954 France's move would be tested, as some top drivers abandoned the series after being penalized. In the Daytona Beach race, Tim Flock finished first but was disqualified when his carburetor was declared illegal during inspection. Flock was so disgusted that he quit the sport. Brother Fonty Flock also left NASCAR, giving up one of the best rides on the circuit, a Frank Christian Oldsmobile. In June 1953 Al Keller, a two-time winner in the 1953 season, defected to the AAA to run open-wheel cars. Late in the year, popular driver Hershel McGriff announced he would retire from racing to pursue a business career.

Increased inspections led to short tempers, and even caused Tim and Fonty Flock to leave the sport. For years many would claim that the rules, when enforced, were not always enforced equally among drivers. **International Motorsports Hall of Fame**

These defections were the realization of one of France's fears. France always believed that fans paid to watch certain popular drivers week in and week out, but if the drivers left, so might the fans. It was to be a conflict of will power, and France kept his powder dry and forged ahead. He had compromised in the past, and would do so again in the future, but this was a time to hold his ground.

Without a doubt, the loss of popular drivers hurt NASCAR, but there was good news as well. New exposure was gained through the new media of television. Three shows—*Desert Dust* out of Phoenix, *Autorama* out of Connecticut, and *Wire Wheels* out of New York—all introduced stock car racing to the public. In fact, *Wire Wheels'* first show was made up of coverage at Daytona Speed Week.

This type of publicity was just what France needed to make the idea of sponsorship more attractive to large corporations. Pure Oil Company, which had introduced the first racing tire for competitors, continued its association with NASCAR. General Textile Mills introduced a new type of helmet for the drivers. Treesdale Laboratories introduced

fire-resistant coveralls. All are early examples of companies getting involved in racing for promotional purposes. They were also early steps toward the refinement of both cars and equipment.

There were 37 races in the 1954 season. Perseverance paid off for Lee Petty, who won his first championship after finishing second, third, fourth, third, and second in the 1949 through 1953 seasons. After driving Plymouths and Dodges, Petty was now in a Chrysler.

Despite Petty's success, Hudson continued to dominate the sport. Out of 37 races, Hudson won 17 times. Oldsmobile was second in wins with 11. Mopar clocked in with a total of 8 wins, as Chryslers won 7 times, and Dodge won once. In the 1954 season Jaguar became the only foreign make ever to win a race, winning a 100-mile event in Lincoln, New Jersey.

1955

Expectations were high for NASCAR as the 1955 season started, but no one could have predicted what a terrible

Lee Petty had played bridesmaid to the champion from 1949 to 1953, but in 1954 he finally won the championship in his 1954 Chrysler. *International Motorsports Hall of Fame*

and difficult year it would be for auto racing. AAA open-wheel drivers were dying with horrifying regularity. Bill Vukovich, Larry Crockett, Mike Nazaruk, Jack McGrath, Jerry Hoyt, and Manuel Ayulo were all killed in race cars.

However, the biggest blow to auto racing in 1955 occurred not in America, but in Europe. On June 1, at the 24 Hours of LeMans, a Mercedes driven by Pierre Levegh lost control, vaulted over a dirt wall and a fence into the crowd. Levegh and nearly 100 spectators were killed. Racers know the risks they take when they climb into the car, but the loss of spectators was much harder to swallow. Many countries, manufacturers, and sanctioning bodies began rethinking their positions on racing.

Indeed, all racing in America was in jeopardy. On July 12, Oregon Senator Richard Neuberger urged President Dwight Eisenhower to outlaw all forms of automobile racing in a passionate but misguided speech to the Senate.

Citing the fatalities in its own events and the tragedy at LeMans, the AAA shocked the racing community when it announced that at the end of the 1955 season, after 54 years of successfully sanctioning the Indianapolis 500 and many other forms of racing, AAA would completely remove itself from automobile racing.

Despite the tragedies, the dramatic events of 1955 left France in an excellent competitive position, as NASCAR was, for all intents and purposes, left alone in the stock car sanctioning business. But France would have to work very hard to capitalize. In an environment where many Americans thought racing should be stopped, France stuck to his guns, and many stayed with him. The sensationalism began to quiet down, and slowly everyone got back to racing.

Automakers also stayed with France and began to tout their NASCAR successes in their advertising. Chrysler ran a two-page ad in national magazines featuring Lee Petty and

Kiekhaefer's help, Chrysler took over from Hudson as the dominant Grand National car.

The success of Kiekhaefer's Chrysler offered proof positive that winning on Sunday meant selling on Monday. Sales of Chryslers were up, and Ford and Chevrolet were concerned. Their response was to set up factory teams to put their brands ahead of the Chryslers.

Hudson dropped to 1 win in 1955, while Chrysler won a total of 27 times. Dodge won once, Ford twice, and

family—Richard Petty was in the racing press three years before he drove a NASCAR race. Chevrolet followed suit, with more than 15,000 billboards and ads in more than 7,000 newspapers associating itself with NASCAR. The major manufacturers were jumping on board, and "Big Bill" France had to be both relieved and happy.

The technology applied to Grand National cars took another step forward in 1955 when a man named Carl Kiekhaefer showed up to race. Kiekhaefer, a Wisconsin native, had been very successful with the Mercury Outboard Motor Company. He ventured into racing primarily to sell boat motors, making him one of the first to use racing as a business proposition to sell a nonautomotive product. He won the first race he entered, at the Daytona Beach Road course, with driver Tim Flock (who, by the way, had cooled off and decided to come back to NASCAR).

Kiekhaefer is generally recognized as the first owner to bring a more formal, scientific approach to the sport. At the time people thought he was crazy, but Kiekhaefer laid the foundation for all future crew chiefs with his attention to every little detail. He brought a weatherman to the race to record the temperature and humidity. He required crew members to document exactly what they did as they worked on the race car. He analyzed the dirt composition of each track. He was also the first to bring his race cars to the track in a covered trailer, the first example of what would come to be known as transporters.

Kiekhaefer's perfectionism produced impressive results. Flock won the championship in Kiekhaefer's Chrysler, entering 38 of the season's 45 races and winning 18 of them. He also recorded an incredible 32 top-five finishes. With

In 1955 Chrysler took over as the most winning brand. Mopar products had enjoyed limited success in the first few years of competition, winning 19 times from 1950 to 1954. In 1955 Chrysler won 27 times and Dodge once for 28 combined wins. The rise of the Chryslers in the mid-1950s was largely due to Carl Kiekhaefer. Kiekhaefer is generally recognized as the first to bring a scientific approach to Grand National racing. His team took weather readings and dirt samples from each track and recorded any change they made to the car. He also ran multiple teams and was the first to bring his cars to the track on a covered hauler. Kiekhaefer got into racing to promote sales of his Mercury Outboards. His plan backfired in a strange way. He was so successful that the fans began to boo when they saw his cars. After a short and very successful venture into the sport he quit, fearing that if fans booed his cars they would not buy his boat motors. *International Motorsports Hall of Fame*

It took the 1955 model to finally get Chevrolet to victory lane in NASCAR's premier series. The 1955 Chevy sported a small-block V-8 engine that would become legendary with both racers and consumers. Chevrolet did not win a race from 1950 to 1954 with its OHV 6 and played second fiddle to their General Motors brother Oldsmobile, which used V-8 power. In 1955 and 1956, Chevy scored 5 total wins, but in 1957 they soared to 21 wins. *International Motorsports Hall of Fame*

General Motors' products won 14 times. Oldsmobile was still the hot General Motors model with 10 wins. Both Buick and Chevrolet gained their first wins in 1955. Both makes backed up their wins, as both ended the season with 2 wins.

Chevy introduced the small-block in 1955. It was a 265-cubic-inch V-8 rated at about 225 horsepower. Chevrolet's first win took place on a half-mile dirt track in Columbia, South Carolina, when Fonty Flock drove his 1955 Chevrolet to victory. The second win came in the year's big race, when Herb Thomas lapped the field in his 1955 Chevrolet to win the Southern 500. Buick's first win came in Charlotte on the old three-quarter-mile dirt track, when Buck Baker's 1955 Buick outran Tim Flock's Chrysler to the checkered flag.

1956

In 1956 Carl Kiekhaefer's methods continued to be a sign of things to come. He entered anywhere from one to six cars in each race. He continued to have Tim Flock in one of his cars, he brought Buck Baker on board, and his third primary driver was Speedy Thompson. With these three talented drivers, his scientific approach, and his powerful Chryslers, Kiekhaefer began to dominate. And it cost him.

Kiekhaefer's success ultimately ended his racing program. His most successful streak was a run of 16 consecutive

wins, a record that will probably never be broken by any car owner. His cars were so successful that the fans tired of seeing the same winners week after week. Both his cars and his drivers were being booed at the track. Kiekhaefer feared that if the fans didn't like his car, they wouldn't like his boat motors either. At the end of the season he pulled his teams out of the sport.

One of NASCAR's competitors was removed in 1956 when a competing sanctioning body, the Society of Autosports and Fellowship Education, merged with NASCAR. A product of this merger was the NASCAR-sanctioned Convertible Division, which held 47 races in 1956.

The Grand National schedule ballooned to 56 races. Buck Baker drove in 48 races to win his first championship, winning 14 times while driving both Chryslers and Dodges. Herb Thomas finished second, with 5 wins out of 48 starts, while driving the relatively new Chevrolets. Speedy Thompson finished third in the championship, driving in 42 races and winning 8 times. Like Baker, he drove both Dodges and Chryslers.

Nineteen fifty-six was an off year for General Motors. GM managed 3 wins, all by Chevrolets. It was the first year Oldsmobile had been shut out since the series began. Meanwhile, Ford products were coming on strong, with Ford winning 14 races and Mercury 3.

Mopar again dominated the series, winning 59 percent of the races. Dodge won 11 times and Chrysler won 22. The Chrysler 300 was the best Mopar ride, considered by many people to be the first true musclecar. It was heavy, weighing in at a bit over 4,000 pounds, but it had a good motor. In 1955 it had 331-cubic-inch engine that put out around 300 horsepower.

By 1956 Chrysler had a 354-cubic-inch V-8 that was rated at 340 horsepower. The engine featured hemispherical combustion chambers in its heads and two four-barrel carburetors. It is considered by many to be the first American production vehicle to achieve more than one horsepower per cubic inch of displacement.

Because the factories were getting more involved in racing, NASCAR had to work to make sure the cars stayed stock. An example of this was in the fourth race of the 1956 season, a 100-mile affair on a paved, half-mile track in West Palm Beach, Florida. Joe Weatherly crossed the finish line first in his 1956 Ford. Jim Reed was next in a 1955 Chevrolet, followed by Herb Thomas in a 1956 Chevrolet. But postrace inspections revealed that Weatherly's car had an illegal camshaft, and there was evidence of grinding and polishing the interior surface of the intake manifold. Second-place driver Jim Reed was then declared the winner, until it was discovered that his Chevy had illegal valves. Two days after the race, Herb Thomas was finally declared the winner. The inspection clampdown was getting tighter.

Here Lee Petty tangles with Ralph Moody on the sands of Daytona in 1956. Dodge offered numerous little frills for the racers, including a high-performance, dual-carburetor setup. It was these "factory options" that gave both racer and street driver more and more power. *International Motorsports Hall of Fame*

1957

Billy Myers gets ready to race in his 1956 Mercury, a car that won 3 races in 1956. Aside from a roll bar and a bit fancier paint, these cars were the same as their street counterparts. Ford began to have an impact on the sport in the late 1950s. From 1950 to 1955, Ford products (Ford, Lincoln, and Mercury) only managed 9 wins. They won 14 races in 1956 and 26 in 1957, more than any other make. *International Motorsports Hall of Fame*

The 1957 season actually started on November 11, 1956, at Willow Springs International Raceway in Lancaster, California. Marvin Panch piloted his 1956 Ford to a win over Fireball Roberts on the 2-1/2-mile dirt-road course. Two more races were run in December 1956: one in North Carolina (another win for Panch), and another in Florida (won by Fireball Roberts). In all of these races competitors ran 1956, or earlier, models. The first race run in 1957 was the 39-lap event at the Daytona Beach and Road course on February 17, where the 1957 models made their debut.

Both radio and television covered some of the Daytona action. Purolator bought a two-page ad in *LIFE* magazine to highlight its association with NASCAR. This was exactly the type of press that France wanted for the sport—it was estimated that more than 20 million people saw the advertisement. Another manufacturing giant, Goodyear Tire and

Rubber, began a long association with NASCAR. One of its first moves was to offer a contingency prize to drivers of the top cars finishing on Goodyear tires.

Nineteen fifty-seven was one of the most pivotal years in NASCAR's history. It was a year in which Bill France's managing and public relations skills and his ability to foresee the future would all be tested. He would pass with flying colors. Under great adversity, France kept his still-young association alive and well enough to prosper in the future.

The season started in promising fashion. After dipping their big toes in to test the NASCAR pool, the big Detroit manufacturers had jumped in. Chevrolet, Ford, Pontiac, Plymouth, Mercury, and to some degree Oldsmobile all fielded factory teams.

Much like today, two of the biggest efforts were from Chevrolet and Ford. The drivers on the Chevrolet payroll included Buck Baker, Speedy Thompson, Jack Smith, Rex White, and Frankie Schneider. Ford had Fireball Roberts,

The 1957 season saw an American classic make its appearance. The 1957 Chevrolet (left) was an instant success as Chevy racked up 21 wins. The 1957 Ford (below) edged out Chevrolet with 26 wins. After dominating the previous year, Mopar went winless in 1957. *International Motorsports Hall of Fame Photo left: Don Hunter*

Curtis Turner, Joe Weatherly, Bill Amick, Marvin Panch, and Ralph Moody in their camp. Pontiac began 1957 with Cotton Owens and Banjo Matthews. Mercury had Billy Myers and Jim Paschal. Lee Petty, along with Johnny Allen, raced Oldsmobiles. Joining these "factory teams" were independent owners and drivers whose jobs were suddenly much harder because they didn't have the money or resources of the factory teams.

It is important to remember the involvement of these companies centered on one thing, and it was not a love of racing. Rather, it was a love of automobile sales. NASCAR racing did two things for the manufacturers. First, if a manufacturer won, it could claim its product to be the best. Second, racing was also a way to promote special-performance options, such as beefier suspension components or more powerful engines, to consumers. Accommodating these performance items, the NASCAR rules allowed teams to compete with any features that were offered to the general public.

One of the hot items of 1957 was fuel injection. Chevrolet offered fuel injection in its street cars so Chevy teams could race with it (at least until NASCAR outlawed it on the track).

Not everyone was comfortable with the manufacturers' involvement in stock car racing. The AAA, a group that was more influential in transportation matters in 1957 than it is today, had conveniently forgotten its recent past and decided that it did not particularly like the marriage of automobile advertising and speed.

The manufacturers and NASCAR countered that their racing efforts allowed manufacturers to learn much about their designs and manufacturing methods. In harsh racing environments, mechanical systems were severely tested. Any improvements manufacturers made would improve the longevity, performance, and safety of their street cars.

What made the situation a real pressure cooker was the fact that the some of the directors of the AAA were also executives of automobile companies.

The manufacturers had started the season aligned with NASCAR's logic and had come to race. But the landscape would change quickly, beginning with the May 19 race at Martinsville Speedway, one of the series' few paved tracks. The 500-lap event would end after only 441 laps when leader Billy Myers' Mercury crashed through a retaining wall and injured a number of spectators, one of whom was an eight-year-old boy.

Reports said that all of those injured were in an area off-limits to spectators, but this argument did not matter. As they had following the LeMans crash of 1955, the press and sensationalists again questioned the future of automobile racing.

The manufacturers quickly buckled under the pressure and pulled out of NASCAR. The consensus was that they would stay away from speed-oriented advertising. The factory drivers were suddenly on their own, forced not only to drive, but also to figure out a way to manage their efforts. The independent teams were not hurt as badly, but they did notice that the flow of hand-me-down parts from the over-supplied factory teams dried up.

Without factory support, it was again difficult for the racers to make ends meet. France pumped more money to the drivers with guaranteed purses and, in some cases, travel money. It was a time when France could not be greedy—he had to put seed money back into the sport. France also continued to press each track and promoter to raise purses for their events.

When the dust finally settled on the 1957 season, Buck Baker had won his second championship, becoming the first driver to win back-to-back championships. He competed in 40 of the season's 53 races and won 10 times.

After dominating the 1956 season with 33 wins, Mopar was gone from the winner's circle in 1957. All of the wins were split between General Motors and Ford, as GM edged out Ford with 27 wins to Ford's 26. Pontiac had 2 wins, Oldsmobile had 4, and Chevrolet scored an impressive 21 wins.

Even though it didn't win, the 1957 M355 Mercury was a fine example of the effort that the factories made to classify a race car as a street car. Very few were sold to the public, but enough were sold to classify it as a stock production car. Mercury had part numbers for all of its modifications, which included twin carburetors, an aluminum intake manifold, and a pretty radical cam. With this assistance, the 368-cubic-inch engine was able to produce 355 horsepower.

The factory also installed an aluminum bell housing, a heavy-duty truck clutch and transmission, an improved suspension (including four shocks per wheel), and beefed-up brakes.

General Motors was also searching for speed. In 1957 its V-8 engine was bored to 283 cubic inches and a mechanical fuel-injection system was added. The fuel injection was quickly outlawed by NASCAR.

Chevy's approach was a little different, but many racers favored the little V-8, which weighed less than many of the competitor's engines. Dirt-track cars could afford to be heavier with a low center of gravity, but the circuit was adding more paved tracks. There, the lighter cars handled better, accelerated quicker, and were much easier on tires.

Another great moment in the sport took place on November 25, 1957. Ground was broken for a new track—a monster track—where high speed would be combined with high banks and plenty of room to pass. Daytona International Speedway was born.

1958

Fireball Roberts flexed his driving muscle in 1958, becoming a fan favorite and, many say, the sport's first superstar. While he only raced in 10 races, he won 6 of them, finished in the top-five eight times and in the top-10 on nine occasions.

Fireball was honored for his efforts when the Florida sportswriters named him the Professional Athlete of the Year. However, Lee Petty won the 1958 championship, his second, with 7 wins in 50 starts. He also had 28 top-5 and 44 top-10 wins. Petty, who had abandoned his favored Mopars after the 1956 season to switch to Oldsmobiles, took the lead in points after the second race and kept the lead all year. Mopar was again winless in 1958. Chevrolet took home the most wins with 25, Oldsmobile had 7, and Pontiac 3, giving General Motors a total of 35. Fords were still racing hard and had 16 wins of their own.

The shaky circumstances of the 1957 season carried into 1958 season. It was a tough time for the sport, and all of the competitors faced great financial strains. The factory dollars that disappeared the previous year had not been replaced. Many of the drivers who dominated the first few years of the sport were either retiring or were not nearly as competitive.

But the show went on. On February 23, the last race was run on the Daytona Road and Beach course. Paul Goldsmith won the race in a Smokey Yunick Pontiac with Curtis Turner finishing a close second.

While some of the early greats were leaving the sport, new ones were on the way. At Ashwood Speedway in Bishopville, South Carolina, an 18-year-old driver flipped his limited sportsman racer, landing it in a lake. The driver climbed on the roof of the car, jumped off into the lake, and swam to the bank. Thus, Cale Yarborough made his first start and was officially on the circuit. And, although no one knew it at the time, one of Yarborough's biggest rivals would make his entry soon after: Richard Petty was on his way.

1959

In 1959 the future arrived. France had turned a personal dream into reality. The Daytona International Motor Speedway was ready for action. It is said that the reason that the track is banked 31 degrees is because it is the steepest angle that could be paved. Regardless, France's new facility was like no other. Big Bill France at last had his dream track and it would influence track design forever.

At the time, most NASCAR races were still run on dirt tracks. Darlington was the first paved speedway built specifically for stock car racing. But Daytona was something different altogether. Marvin Panch had said he was retiring from driving, but when he saw Daytona he postponed his retirement because he had to race it. Perhaps driver Jimmy Thompson said it best: "There have been other tracks that separated the men from the boys. This is the track that will separate the brave from the weak after the boys are gone."

The first Daytona 500 took place on February 22, 1959, but before the first race the teams ran two warm-up races. Shorty Rollins gets credit for winning the first race at Daytona when, on February 20, he took the 25-lap Convertible Division Race. Bob Welborn won the next 25-lapper in the Grand National cars.

Then it was time for the big one, the Daytona 500. The lead swapped hands 33 times between seven drivers. Fireball Roberts was hot early, moving from his 46th starting position to the lead in just 23 laps, but he dropped out of the race with a failed fuel pump. Jack Smith led in the middle stages, but went four laps down with tire problems. Bob Welborn also led, but blew his engine on lap 75.

In the closing stages, Lee Petty and Johnny Beauchamp were the only two drivers on the lead lap. They fought for the lead, side by side on the last lap until they crossed the finish line. It took more than four days for NASCAR officials to interpret the photo finish and name Petty the winner.

The purse for the race was more than $67,000, a big improvement for the drivers. The contingencies were getting better, too. For his win, Petty received an additional $5,000 because he was driving a 1959-model car, money that France had offered to anyone who won in a 1959 model.

France knew that demanding all cars be 1959 models would hurt the smaller teams, and would then hurt his chances of filling a starting grid. However, he thought that it was important for the newest cars possible to race. Incidentally, it is said that Lee Petty bought a new Oldsmobile for the race for about $2,500 cash.

Another point of interest at the Daytona track was the presence of Indy cars. USAC had agreed to have a two-hour practice during the February Speed Weeks. Unfortunately, these cars were not ready for the speeds that could be achieved on the heavily banked track. Marshall Teague was killed when he lost control of his car because of aerodynamic lift.

On April 4, the Indy cars were back for a 100-mile race. George Amick was killed on the last lap while battling for third position. USAC officials canceled a scheduled July 4 race, and rightly so, as they understood that the equipment they raced was not ready for the speeds and stress that Daytona put on their cars. They have never been back.

There were 44 races in the 1959 season. Lee Petty followed his historic Daytona 500 win with a third championship, winning 11 races in 42 starts. His first 4 wins came while driving an Oldsmobile, but early in the season he switched back to Mopar products and picked up his last 7 wins in a Plymouth.

The decade came to an end with Chevrolet and Ford both scoring 16 wins. Ned Jarrett took one of these wins for Ford, as he won his first Grand National race on August 1, at Rambi Raceway in Myrtle Beach, South Carolina, driving a 1957 model.

In 1959 the Ford Thunderbird was run on the circuit for the first time. In 1960 Ford would go back to the Galaxie, but the model that would become one of the greatest race cars ever had made its debut. Oldsmobile, with four wins, and Mopar, with seven Plymouth wins, could thank Petty for all of their visits to victory lane.

Opposite and above: In the 50s the cars were primarily running on dirt tracks with the occasional paved one, as these photos from 1953 demonstrate. Dirt-track racing would eventually disappear from the Grand National circuit. Heavy cars worked well on the relatively soft dirt tracks, but on paved tracks they were very hard on tires. Lighter cars would accelerate and decelerate better and were much easier on tires. They would prove to be the way of the future. *International Motorsports Hall of Fame*

Rex White won the 1960 championship in his 1960 Chevrolet, scoring 6 wins in 40 starts. Chevrolets accounted for 13 wins in 1960.
International Motorsports Hall of Fame

Chapter Three

The 1960s

Following the success of the Daytona track, more superspeedways (and a great new paved short track) were being built. Atlanta, North Carolina, Riverside, Rockingham, and Bristol all came online in the early to mid-1960s. Although NASCAR would continue to use dirt tracks throughout the 1960s, the cars began to run more and more on paved tracks, and crew chiefs no longer had to worry as much about running on dirt. The paved tracks allowed more speed than ever before. Another great track was added to the circuit with the completion of the Charlotte Motor Speedway. When the cars showed up to race for the first time on June 19, the track was barely completed.

The paving at Charlotte Motor Speedway was finished just before qualifying began. As a result, the fresh asphalt, which did not have time to set up, was ripped up by the cars.

Even though the track's surface was suspect at best, the race would go on. Teams covered their grilles and windshields with screens in an attempt to protect drivers and engines from the hunks of fresh asphalt flying everywhere. Joe Lee Johnson was best at navigating the potholes and won in his 1960 Chevrolet. More than 35,000 spectators paid to watch the race.

Two more paved tracks entered the schedule in 1960. Marchbanks Speedway, a 1.4-mile banked and paved track, was built in Hanford, California, by B. L. Marchbanks. California driver Marvin Porter won the June 12 race at this new track. The prize money for the event was not lucrative enough to get the Southern drivers to drag a car all the way to California, so the top drivers had informally decided not to race. They all agreed, except for Rex White. He went to California, finished eighth and collected close to 500 points. This helped Rex win the 1960 championship.

The Atlanta International Raceway was also completed and on July 31, 1960, its first race, a 300-miler, was run. Fireball Roberts took the checkered flag.

France was also happy in 1960 when CBS came to Daytona. The network broadcast the Grand National Pole races live, but wasn't ready to show the 500-miler, figuring it was far too long. But CBS was not the only network to go racing. On February 12, NBC broadcast a 10-mile invitational race on the *Today Show*. This early exposure was the first step toward visually reaching the fans who were not at the track.

Another big story of 1960 was the man who finished second to Rex White in the points battle. Richard Petty ran 40 races, the same number as White, and won 3 of them. He had 30 top-10 finishes and 16 top-5 finishes. After only a couple of years on the circuit, Richard Petty was quickly becoming a force.

NASCAR underwent a major administrative change in 1960. Erwin G. "Cannonball" Baker died at the age of 78. He had held the position of NASCAR commissioner since 1948. His successor was none other than Harley Earl, a former vice president of General Motors. It was an appointment that offered many Detroit connections.

There were 44 races in the 1960 season. As the 1960s began, the General Motors vs. Ford battle continued. Ford won 15 races in 1960 with hot drivers including young Ned Jarrett, Glen Wood, Joe Weatherly, and Speedy Thompson. Once again, Mercury and Lincoln failed in their attempts to

visit victory lane. Chevrolet had 13 wins and Pontiac 7. Dodge won once and Plymouth 8 times to give Mopar a respectable total of 9 wins.

1961

By 1961 the sport was changing and its image was beginning to be an issue. NASCAR's early competitors were often a little rough around the edges. For many years the commonly held image of stock car racers was of uneducated southerners who raced when they were not hauling moonshine. There was some truth to this, as these were the roots of the sport.

But as the sport got bigger, more racers began to race for a living instead of as a sideline. Following this trend, sponsorship became more of an issue for the teams and drivers. For companies to want to do large sponsorship deals, they needed to be associated with a more comfortable image. Richard Petty would ultimately set the blueprint for this area. He was country, southern, and a gentleman.

There were still a great number of weekend warriors during the 1950s, but as the 1960s got under way this began to change. First, the cars were becoming more and more of an investment. While they were still derived from production cars, more and more modifications were necessary to compete. The top teams and drivers had their acts together. They may not have been very polished, but they were cunning and very proficient in mechanical skills.

The big story of 1961 was not the power struggle on the track. Rather, it was the power struggle between Curtis Turner, Bill France, the drivers, and a union. In financing issues over the new Charlotte Motor Speedway, Turner, the first president of the track, had turned to the Teamsters Union for some critical speedway financing. The union was interested, but in return it hoped to associate the sport's popular, well-known drivers with the union. This ultimately led to the Federation of Professional Athletes, a stand-alone union with some ties to the Teamsters. Turner heavily lobbied drivers to join and signed quite a few, promising better purses, better benefits, and a pension.

Big Bill France was livid. He vowed not to allow Teamsters to race and said that it was a policy that he would enforce with a pistol if necessary. He also stated that he would plow up the Daytona facility and plant corn before he would allow union racers to compete. Some hard heads were about to butt. Curtis Turner, Tim Flock, and Fireball Roberts were all immediately suspended for life from NASCAR for their association with the union.

The battle was on as each side fired statements at the other. France did understand, to some degree, the concerns that drove the drivers to unionize. After all, he was a former driver himself. He knew that some compromise had to be made, so he formed the Grand National Advisory Board. It was a council made up of two drivers, two owners, two promoters, and two NASCAR executives.

This move allowed everyone involved in the process of racing to have their voices heard, and France showed that NASCAR was willing to listen. Soon the drivers who joined the union began to defect. In the end, Big Bill won the war. The drivers who were suspended for life were allowed to reenter the NASCAR world, and everyone got back to the business of racing.

Ned Jarrett won the 1961 championship, starting 46 events. Ned won only 1 race, a 100-mile event on a half-mile dirt track in Birmingham, Alabama. Rex White won 7 races in 47 starts, and Joe Weatherly won an impressive 9 races in only 25 starts. Despite only 1 win, Jarrett was consistent week in and week out, and it won him the championship.

The new, wider Pontiac made a statement in 1961. It dominated, winning 31 of the season's 52 races. The car was not made wider for handling purposes, but so that it could fit more motor and accessories under the hood. The car's better handling was just a side benefit.

Chevrolet also helped the General Motors effort with 11 wins of its own. Ford found it difficult to keep pace with General Motors in 1961. Mercury and Lincoln were shut out again, and Ford registered only 7 wins. It was also a low year for Mopar. Chrysler won 1 race and Plymouth 2, giving Mopar a scant 3 wins.

1962

In June 1962, Ford became the first automaker to break the 1957 Automobile Manufacturers Association's ban on participation in automobile racing. In truth, the ban had always been only skin deep. Automakers still knew that winning on the track meant better sales. While they did not publicly support racing programs, the latest cars with the latest motors and the latest options still found their way to the track.

Henry Ford II himself wrote that the ban no longer had purpose or effect and stated that Ford was ignoring the ban. Within a month, Chrysler too had forgotten the ban and had jumped back into racing, publicly supporting its racing teams. General Motors would prove to be the slowest of the big three to come around.

The 1962 season had a total of 53 races. Joe Weatherly won the championship with 9 wins, an impressive 39 top-5 finishes, and 45 top-10 finishes. Richard Petty finished second in the championship, with Ned Jarrett third.

The following story exemplifies the effort that helped win the championship for Weatherly. On May 6, the Grand National tour was in Concord, North Carolina, at the Concord Speedway, a half-mile dirt track. Weatherly qualified seventh and ran well all day. He was running second to Richard Petty when Petty broke an axle. It looked like

It was common for older models to continue to race for a few years. Elmo Langley drove this 1959 Pontiac Catalina in the 1961 Daytona 500. *International Motorsports Hall of Fame*

smooth sailing for Weatherly, but with 50 laps to go the throttle on his car hung in the wide-open position. Weatherly quickly turned the car off and coasted it through the turn.

After surviving the turn, he decided not to pull into the pits. Instead, he turned the engine back on and shot down the straightaway. Once again he turned the car off entering the turn and coasted through. This would be Weatherly's driving style for the last 50 laps. He went on to win the race in a display of skill at both driving and adaptation.

General Motors continued to dominate the winner's circle in 1962. Pontiac again scored more wins than any other make with 22. The hot Pontiac ride was the 1962 Catalina. The car began life as a stock body shipped from the factory straight to the team's shop without an engine, drivetrain, or suspension. It had a 120-inch wheelbase and weighed 3,835 pounds. The suspension had twin shocks and the springs were fitted with jackscrews, or upper mounts, that allowed

Above: With the success of the General Motors models, Ford was limited to seven wins in 1961. Here, Fred Lorenzen gets a tow back to the garage after an accident in the 1961 Dixie 400 at Atlanta. *International Motorsports Hall of Fame*

Right: Pontiac had great success in the early 1960s with their Catalina, which was a great-handling car for its time. Pontiac scored seven wins in 1960, 31 in 1961, 22 in 1962 and 5 in 1963. Here Mexican Formula 1 driver Pedro Rodriguez prepares to take a turn behind the wheel of a 1963 Pontiac Catalina stock car in the 1963 "Firecracker 400." *International Motorsports Hall of Fame*

Chevrolet added seven wins to the 1963 General Motors campaign. Left, Junior Johnson heads out to practice in his 1963 Chevrolet. *International Motorsports Hall of Fame*

Johnny Rutherford came over from the open-wheel ranks and drove this Smokey Yunick–prepared Pontiac (below) to victory in a 100-mile race at Daytona in 1963. *International Motorsports Hall of Fame*

them to be fine-tuned. The spring sits under a fitting, which is welded to a large bolt. This bolt then passes through a threaded fitting in the frame of the car. If the bolt is tightened, the spring pressure is increased. If it is loosened, the spring rate decreases. This allows racers to fine-tune each spring on the car—commonly referred to as "adjusting the wedge." A 421-cubic-inch overhead valve V-8 rated at more than 400 horsepower supplied power. The cars ran more than 156 miles per hour at Daytona.

Chevrolet also had a strong year, adding 14 wins to give General Motors a total of 36. Ford again had a mediocre year, scoring only 6 wins. With Richard Petty behind the wheel, Plymouth began to come on strong, and Mopar finished the 1962 season with 11 wins.

1963

The 1963 season began on November 4, 1962, at Birmingham Speedway in Birmingham, Alabama. Three races would be run in 1962, so teams ran 1962-model-year cars. The 1963 models were not unveiled until January 20, 1963, at Riverside, California. Even though Ford and

Chrysler had begun to publicly support racing again, General Motors continued its ban into the 1963 season. However, its products were still winning, and there was some factory support.

The 1963 season was another marathon. Fifty-five races were run, and Joe Weatherly won another championship, competing in 52 races and winning 3 times. Richard Petty somehow finished second in the championship, despite running in 54 races and winning 14 times.

The return of factory support upped the competition both on the track and in the shops. The race to find better

continued on page 63

The Body

In the early years, race car bodies were simply what the factory provided. Roll bars were not required until the mid-1950s, so the body provided the only protection the driver had. One of the few modifications allowed was a hood strap to keep the hood from flying back to block the driver's view. *International Motorsports Hall of Fame*

The importance of a Winston Cup car's body profile has grown, especially in the last three decades of racing. The horsepower wars have leveled out, forcing the teams to look for advantages in the suspension and body. Readily available aftermarket parts and a workforce that sees engine builders moving from team to team have resulted in fairly even horsepower numbers throughout the field.

By tuning the aerodynamics of the bodies, the teams can reduce drag and increase downforce. The most critical Winston Cup bodies are those on the superspeedway cars. Because a superspeedway car is fitted with a power-robbing restrictor plate on the engine, the efficiency with which a car moves through the air determines the car's top speed. At other tracks the car's body shape will be focused on downforce, which is the pressure exerted on the body by the air

flowing over it, causing the entire car to be "pushed" down onto the track. This helps the car stick in the turns and allows higher speeds. While downforce helps in the turns, it creates drag when the car goes down the straightaway.

Some say that the body profile is not very critical at short tracks and road courses, but the truth is that if the wheels are rolling, aerodynamics matter.

On a modern Cup car the roof skin, the hood skin, and the rear deck lid skin are the only stock body parts. The rest of the body, with the exception of the front and rear bumper covers, is handmade and hand-assembled.

In the 1950s simple roll bars were installed to keep the roof from caving in during rollovers. Proper safety equipment was still a long time away— luckily, the short dirt tracks of the day kept speeds relatively low. *International Motorsports Hall of Fame*

sions of the templates and a car must comply if it is to race.

Body construction begins at the top of the car and proceeds downward. This means the roof skin is usually the first piece to go on. By knowing how high the top of the car is supposed to be when it is completed, builders can mount the roof template over the car to use as a guide when building the body.

Airflow over the roof is also of critical importance. How the air flows off the roof, rear window, and over the deck lid influences the way the air hits the rear spoiler, which in turn affects the way the car handles. Teams go to great lengths to make sure the airflow to the rear spoiler is optimized while still ensuring that the roof profile remains legal.

Teams also use the factory-produced hood from the make and model of the car being raced. However, the original support panels that hold the sheet-metal hood rigid are replaced with custom supports. A good hood profile is necessary for good airflow over the car. On longer tracks, if the

Fenders, quarter panels, the sides of the car, and many other small body pieces are handmade from standard sheet metal. The compound curves in these pieces are very difficult to make and require a great deal of experience to make them quickly and uniformly. Mechanical rollers and English wheels are used to give each part its final contours.

The body must withstand the tremendous air pressure of racing at 200 miles per hour on a superspeedway or the "fender banging" so common during short-track racing. The body will deflect debris and withstand some damage, but the driver relies on the roll cage for protection.

The body must accomplish another, less dangerous task. It must fit the template. From the beginning of the building of the body until its inspection before the race, the templates rule the body. Templates are standardized aluminum patterns defining the pro-file of the car's body. NASCAR establishes the dimen-

The modern Winston Cup car shares very little with its stock brother. By the mid-1990s the only stock body pieces on the car were the hood skin, roof skin, and part of the deck lid.

From the beginning of the car-building process, the template rules the assembly. Since the template will judge the car during inspection before the race, the builders keep an eye on their tolerances throughout the building process, as the body is welded and riveted onto the chassis.

Grille openings are also used to duct air to the brake rotors when racing on tracks that are demanding on brakes (mainly short tracks and road courses). Air is also ducted from the left side of the grille opening to the oil cooler, which is mounted inside the left front fender in front of the tire. Overheating of these systems is likely if these openings are closed due to damage or debris.

At the bottom of the front bumper cover is the air dam. The air dam's purpose is to keep as much air from going under the car as possible. The more air that goes under the car, the more drag and lift the car will have. As the car goes faster, the lift increases. If the air dam is damaged, the car is likely to be slower and more difficult to drive.

hood is damaged, the disturbance of this airflow will dramatically slow a race car. Short-track performance is usually not affected by cosmetic damage.

The bumper covers are not the same pieces that are used on production cars. These "one-piece" units are produced for racing purposes only. Since aerodynamics have become so important, the dimensions and shape of the bumper covers are established before the season begins to ensure that no model gains an unfair advantage by converting the multiple-piece production bumper to a one-piece racing unit.

All bumper covers must have a serial number (which must remain visible), and their shape cannot be altered to improve aerodynamic flow. The front bumper cover is mounted on a frame of square tubing, which is fabricated during the building of the chassis.

The grille area of the front bumper cover is of critical importance and must do a number of things simultaneously. As the leading edge of the car, the bumper cover is a determining factor in the car's aerodynamic efficiency. Grilles must allow enough air to enter to cool the engine, but too large an opening will create drag and will also lift the front end of the car at high speeds, affecting the car's handling.

The rear bumper covers are manufactured much the same as the front bumper covers. The original equipment manufacturer and NASCAR officials establish the rear bumper cover's specifications, keeping the profile and shape roughly the same as that of the production car. The rear bumper cover is a one-piece construction that does not include a functional bumper.

handling and generate more horsepower was on. But a problem loomed on the horizon. Much more time was being spent making the cars faster than making the drivers safer in their cars. This would soon prove fatal.

In 1963 the win meter began to swing away from GM and back to Ford and Mopar. The Plymouths continued to get stronger, with 19 wins. Fords took 23 checkered flags and Mercury took 1. The Ford Galaxie was proving to be a tough competitor with the aid of its 427-cubic-inch motor. This mill not only had cubic inches, it also used a single four-barrel carburetor, an aluminum intake manifold, and cast-iron headers to produce more than 400 horsepower.

General Motors accounted for only 10 wins in 53 races, with Chevrolet winning 7 times, and Pontiac winning 3. The 1963 Chevy Impala, even with the General's AMA ban in place, came up with a "race-only" 427-cubic-inch engine that was kept as secret as possible. Smokey Yunick and Junior Johnson were so taken with the engine's power that they jumped on board with Chevrolet immediately.

The pressure of the AMA ban caused the engines to be recalled, but the racers protested and the engines were eventually made available to the teams. However, the factory stopped R&D on the 427, and parts were very limited. The result was an extremely powerful motor that qualified well and raced well until it blew up.

The 427 cars often started up front, but they seldom finished a race. The car qualified at more than 165 miles per hour at Daytona, which was 8 miles per hour faster than the previous year's qualifying effort.

1964

After a few seasons with limited success, Mopar was coming on strong. In 1963 Chrysler brought back the hemi

and a double rocker arm valvetrain. The new motor was awesome. At Daytona, Richard Petty's Dodge ran a lap at more than 174 miles per hour. A year earlier he had only been able to muster about 155 miles per hour. Petty went on to win the Daytona 500 and Mopars finished first, second, and third.

But the horsepower wars were having bad side effects. Power and speed had increased, but the cars' safety systems had not. Joe Weatherly died in a crash at Riverside. It is speculated that his head hit the wall on impact and his helmet was not enough to protect him. Weatherly was also driving without a shoulder harness.

The hot ride in 1963 proved to be the Ford Galaxie. Ford had packed into the car a potent 427-cubic-inch engine that produced over 400 horsepower. Ford won 23 times in 1963 to become the winningest manufacturer. *International Motorsports Hall of Fame*

By the mid-1960s the cars were much more streamlined and powerful than they were in the 50s. Drivers like Bobby Isaac and Richard Petty often drove Chrysler Corporation cars to victory lane in the mid-1960s. *International Motorsports Hall of Fame*

Fireball Roberts was the next fatality. His crash at Charlotte involved Junior Johnson and Ned Jarrett. Roberts was pulled from his burning car by Jarrett and taken to the hospital. For a while it looked like Roberts would survive, but he died as a result of his injuries about five weeks after the accident.

With all of the power that Chrysler motors were putting out, Ford had to do something. Many said that Ford was dramatically lightening the bodies of its cars—a move that further hurt safety. Plymouth driver Jimmy Pardue lost his life on the track. During a tire test at Charlotte, a blowout put his car into the fence. Pardue died in the hospital hours after the accident.

While all agreed that safety should be first, there was argument on how to do it. There had been talk of dropping the maximum engine displacement from 428 cubic inches to 396 cubic inches to reduce speeds.

NASCAR eventually decided that the engine displacement would stay at 428 cubic inches for 1965, but that many of the "special" items that were put into race engines, such as overhead cams, high-risers, and hemispherical heads,

would be banned. The new rules hurt the Mopar guys the most. The powerful engines they had developed and now relied upon were useless. As a result, Chrysler boycotted much of the 1965 Grand National season.

The 1964 season had 62 races. General Motors, still hesitant to get back into stock car racing officially, managed

Tires were still a problem in the mid-1960s. With higher and higher speeds being reached in the heavy stock cars, the heat build-up was often too much for the tires. When they failed, it was usually at high speed and often in a turn. Losing a right-front tire most often meant a hard right turn into the wall.
International Motorsports Hall of Fame

only 1 win in 1964 when a Chevrolet driven by Wendell Scott won the third race of the year at a half-mile dirt track in Jacksonville, Florida. Ford products dominated with 30 wins from Ford and 5 from Mercury. The Galaxie was still running strong. Mopar products, with their big hemi engines, also had a good year with Dodge winning 14 times and Plymouth winning 3.

1965

Because of the deaths in 1964, safety was the big issue for 1965. Joe Weatherly, Fireball Roberts, and Jimmy Pardue had all been killed. However, a number of problems made a quick fix very difficult.

First, the cars had lots of horsepower but they had poor aerodynamics and very basic suspensions. As the cars got faster, they became more difficult for the driver to control.

Tires were also becoming a problem. Because of the increase in speed, the tires were put under greater stress and, as a result, more and more heat was generated in the tires. Heat is the real enemy of tires, causing them to fall apart more often.

For the 1965 season NASCAR, introduced new rules to slow cars and improve safety. Engine displacement was limited to a maximum of 428 cubic inches. There would be no

more hemispherical combustion chambers, high-rise cylinder heads, roller cams, or roller tappets. Only one four-barrel carburetor would be allowed and it would be restricted to a maximum barrel diameter of 1-11/16 inches. NASCAR would also mandate that the cars use a longer wheelbase on superspeedways.

The cars of the mid-1960s were much stronger than the cars from the previous decade. Roll bars, better helmets and more preparation were giving drivers a better chance to escape an accident without injury. Here a Mercury Marauder is prepared for the track.
International Motorsports Hall of Fame

The big block was Detroit's answer to the need for more horsepower. Today's engines are limited to 358 cubic inches, but the big blocks were well over 400. Chrysler Corporation had its 426-cubic-inch motors, Chevrolet had the 427, and Ford fielded both the 427, like the example shown here, and the 429.

Chrysler was hit hard with the ban on the hemi, and Ford could not run its high-rise engines. Ford didn't mind the rules changes all that much, taking the attitude that it would be a practical way to do some R&D on stock-type components. Chrysler, however, was quite upset. Ultimately, it would mean less Mopar support for stock car racing.

Chrysler vowed to pull out of NASCAR for 1965 and run in USAC, SCCA, NHRA, and IMCA, where the hemi heads were still legal. France decided to ride out the Mopar boycott, hoping that General Motors would abandon its "no racing" policy and come back to the track to offset the loss of Chrysler. But in December 1964, GM Vice President Lewis Goad announced that GM would not return to racing.

France defended the rule changes. He felt the performance of the cars was getting out of hand, and that something had to be done to give the drivers a chance. He wanted strong factory participation, but if he did not create some limits, the manufacturers would ultimately show up with 500-cubic-inch motors. Aside from the need to cut speeds, France wanted to keep the sport as close as possible to its stock roots.

As a result, 1965 was shaping up to be an all-Ford season (it had announced earlier that it would only be giving factory support to teams running in NASCAR). At Daytona,

Ford and Mercury took the first 13 finishing positions. Meanwhile, USAC would be all Chrysler.

After the clampdown on Mopar engines, Richard Petty left the circuit. He decided to go drag racing instead, but his effort ended with terrible results. At a dragway in Dallas, Petty lost control of his car during a run. The car hit a dirt bank, flew in the air, and landed among some spectators. An eight-year-old boy was killed and seven others were injured.

NASCAR would explore other safety improvements besides limiting power. One was the rubber-lined fuel cell, initially made by Firestone. Cars had previously run regular metal tanks that were prone to split open in wrecks and spill fuel everywhere. When the metal exterior of the new, rubber-lined tank was damaged, the fuel would remain in the tank, secure in the flexible rubber bladder.

Goodyear introduced the Goodyear Lifesaver Inner Tire, the predecessor to the modern inner liner. While the tire could still blow, the inner tire would give some support and allow the driver to slow before the rim could dig into the track and possibly cause the car to flip.

But in France's big picture, things were getting worse for NASCAR. As the season progressed, attendance was down at the tracks, and track owners were becoming restless.

The Ford Galaxie ruled in 1965. The car handled reasonably well and the motor, still the 427 powerplant, was very powerful. Ford won an incredible 48 of 55 races in 1965. This was helped by the fact that General Motors had stopped factory support of stock car racing, and many GM teams had switched to Fords. *International Motorsports Hall of Fame*

Chevrolets were still being run by a few teams, but they did not do all that well. By the time summer rolled around France knew that he had to do something, and that something was to institute more rules.

One new rule for the 1965 season connected cubic inches to car weight. Following the World 600 race on June 21, a minimum weight of 9.36 pounds per cubic inch of engine would be enforced. That meant a car with a 427 engine had to weigh 3,996.72 pounds, but a car with a 358-cubic-inch engine could weigh 3,350.88 pounds.

NASCAR also relented on the hemi engines. They were to be allowed in the Plymouth Fury, Dodge 880, and Dodge Polara on tracks over 1 mile. On tracks less than 1 mile, or on road courses, they could be run in the Plymouth

continued on page 71

The Suspension

The cars of the 1950s relied on their stock suspensions. Teams were allowed to use heavy-duty axles but the rest of the suspension was the same as what the factory offered. First this was the straight stock consumer suspension. Later, the manufacturers began to offer "severe usage kits," which consisted of beefed-up suspension parts. These were only able to pass the strictly stock rule by having factory part numbers and being offered for sale to the general public. *International Motorsports Hall of Fame*

Over the years, leaf springs like the ones shown here, torsion bars, and coil spring suspensions have all been successful, but by the 1970s coil springs had pretty much taken over suspension duties on stock cars. *International Motorsports Hall of Fame*

Handling is where it's at. When on the track there are few things in Winston Cup racing as important as a properly tuned suspension. Early racers had to rely on stock suspensions, but today's racers can make an almost infinite number of adjustments to refine the car's handling. The individual suspension components that are selected and how they are adjusted determines the "suspension setup." These setups are the difference between the cars that handle well and win and those that don't handle so well and don't win.

There is no doubt that horsepower will get you down the straightaway faster, but the truth is that horsepower is reasonably close between all of the top teams. As a result, the winning race car is the one that gets through the corners the fastest. A prime demonstration of this fact occurred after a restrictor plate was added to the cars at the second race at New Hampshire in 2000. The plate decreased horsepower from more than 750 to about 460 (about a 40 percent drop). However, the pole qualifying speed dropped less than 5 miles per hour, from 132.089 to 127.632, or 3.4 percent. It is speed through the turns that makes for fast lap times. Take 40 percent of the spring rate out of the car and the speeds would really drop.

The suspensions on all makes of Winston Cup cars are the same. On the front suspension, control arms or A-frames (they are shaped like the letter A when viewed from below) form the main link between the chassis and the suspension. On each side, the

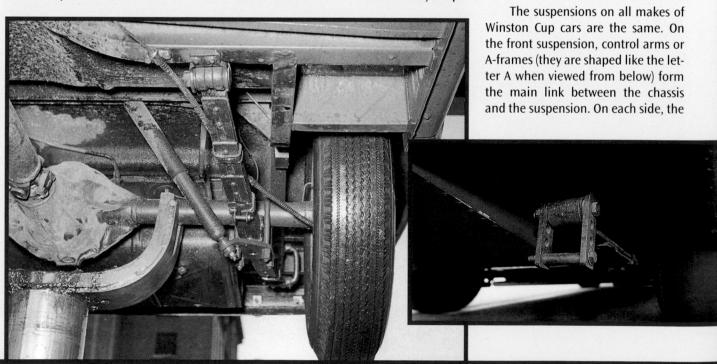

the trailing arms attach to the rear axle and have fixtures to connect the rear shock absorbers and the rear springs, which are mounted between the trailing arms and the frame.

Modern Winston Cup cars use coil springs on both the front and rear suspensions. On the rear suspension, the upper and lower coil spring mounts must be located between the rear frame side rails. The rear lower mounts must be located on either the rear axle trailing arms or on top of the rear axle housing. The upper mounts must be connected to the chassis directly above the lower mounts.

The primary tool used to set the car up is the selection of the coil springs. Springs are categorized by spring rate, a measure of the resistance a spring exerts when compressed, which is expressed in pounds. Because of the importance of springs in making a car handle well, crews will test many combinations of spring rates on various corners of the car.

On oval tracks, a typical setup calls for a different spring rate at each corner of the car to counter the particular forces that that track applies to the car as it turns. For instance, at Dover the force on the right front tire is about 3,500 pounds, essentially the entire weight of the car, which forces the team to run a 3,500-pound spring in the right front. At a short, flat track there will be much less weight on the right front and the teams will run a much lighter spring, maybe 1,400 pounds.

Even after the team finds the right spring combination of a track, its work is not done. Winston Cup cars are built with fixtures on the upper spring mount that allow teams to tune the springs even finer. These devices are known as jacking bolts or jackscrews. And when they are tightened or loosened they change the weight distribution of the car. Fans often see this done during pit stops. It is

For many years cars ran two shocks to absorb the pounding of the track. But with the introduction of gas shocks, the cars went from two hydraulic shocks to one gas shock. The gas shock gave the teams much more control over the compression and rebound characteristics of each corner of the car.

front coil spring's lower mount is found on the lower control arm. The top of the spring is mounted under the frame. Cup cars use specially manufactured tubular control arms, which are much lighter and stronger than their stock counterparts.

Trailing arms link the chassis and the rear suspension. The fronts of the trailing arms attach to the body with hinged fixtures just aft of the center of the car. The backs of

The modern suspension. In the top photo, notice the shape of the A-arm in the front suspension. You can also see the front spring, painted yellow, as it rests on the A-arm. A close look reveals the steering links and the front sway bar. In the bottom photo, taken from the rear of the car facing forward, the long trailing arms connecting the rear axle to the frame are clearly visible, as are the dark blue springs, which suspend the axle and trailing arms.

most often called "putting wedge in the car" or simply "adjusting the wedge."

Special openings in the rear window allow the rear jack bolts to be turned very quickly during pit stops. However, the hood must be opened to adjust the front springs. Rubber inserts are also allowed between the spring coils to add stiffness to the spring. These can be put in or, more commonly, removed during pit stops to increase or decrease the spring rate.

Another critical tool used to control handling is the shock absorber. Winston Cup cars use heavy-duty aftermarket shocks on each corner of the car. Any shock used must be available to all competitors.

At one time competitors ran two shocks per wheel, but with the recent advances made in shock absorber technology, this is no longer the case. Modern shock absorbers are able to handle the load with just one shock per wheel.

In the last 10 years, teams have begun to spend more and more time finding the perfect shock combination. This combination in great part determines the car's handling characteristics and, thus, its lap times. Shock absorbers are tuned just like most

other parts of the car. A "shock dyno" is used to test the shock's characteristics when it is removed from the car. Teams can fine-tune the shock to achieve the compression and rebound settings they desire.

Other areas that are used to adjust the suspension include the amount of air pressure in tires. Usually 1 pound of additional air pressure in a tire equates to roughly 10 pounds of spring rate. Sway bars function to link the suspension and the chassis. The thicker the sway bar, the tighter the link between the chassis and the suspension. The tighter the link, the less movement there is between the suspension and the chassis, resulting in less "body roll" when the car is turning.

The track bar is used to keep the rear end "square" under the car. As the car goes through the turn the rear end will be twisted in relation to the body. Track or "Panhard" bars are attached at one end to the frame and at the other end to the end of one of the trailing arms. Usually the bar runs from the left side of the body to the right-rear trailing arm. This extra support is critical for stability through the turns. The track bar may be adjusted to refine the handling of the car during both practice and the race.

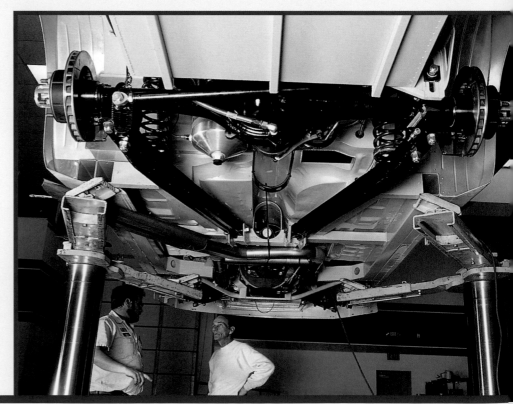

Belvedere and Dodge Coronet. By late July, the Chrysler factory-backed teams were running again (including Richard Petty). Chrysler was still not happy with the super-speedway situation, but at least the hemi could compete.

The long 1965 season had 55 races. Because of the almost complete absence of Mopar and General Motors in 1965, Ford set a record for most consecutive wins with 32, a record that most likely will never be broken. Ford won a total of 48 races and Mercury added 1. Plymouth managed 4 wins and Dodge 2. No General Motors brands won a race.

Ned Jarrett ran in 54 of the season's races, winning 13 of them. He ran away with the Grand National Championship,

winning it by more than 3,000 points over second-place finisher Dick Hutcherson. During the year Curtis Turner also came back into NASCAR racing and ran 7 races.

1966

Nineteen sixty-six started where 1965 left off. The hemi engine had become a production engine and France continued to let them race, but controversy continued. Rules mandated that on superspeedways the hemis could only be used in a Fury or Polara. If the hemi configuration was to be used in one of the smaller Chargers, Belvederes, or Coronets, it had to be dropped from 426 cubic inches to

In 1966 Dodge introduced the shape of things to come. The modern stock car gains performance through engine power, suspension-related handling improvements, and the aerodynamic efficiency of the body. As racers were stuck with stock bodies, the choice of car was very important. The fastback design would soon be offered to teams from many manufacturers, as aerodynamics became more of a factor. Here, David Pearson presents a new Dodge Charger. *International Motorsports Hall of Fame*

405 cubic inches. All of this meant more headaches and more expense for the teams running Dodges or Plymouths.

Ford came out with a new overhead cam engine, but it was a limited-run, nonproduction engine. NASCAR and USAC both outlawed the new motor. Ford finally did get the overhead cam engines into production, but to run them the Ford teams had to comply with a 10.36-pound-per-cubic-inch rule. As this was higher than the 9.36-pound-per-cubic-inch rule, Ford felt that it was getting the short end of the stick. It was Ford's turn to boycott the series, starting on April 15. But this time, probably because everyone was sick of boycotts, the tracks and promoters fully backed NASCAR. France won this round, and by the end of the year Ford was back.

The 1966 Grand National Championship went to David Pearson. Pearson started 42 races, had 15 wins, 26 top-5 finishes, and 33 top-10 finishes. Mopar was back as the dominant manufacturer in 1966. Dodge racked up 18 wins and Plymouth another 16 to give Mopar a total of 34 victories. Ford won 10 times and Mercury twice. Chevrolet also came back to the winner's circle with 3 victories.

1967

Two years of boycotts and controversy had taken their toll on stock car racing. Attendance was down and tempers were short. The show started to get back on track in 1967,

Ford only won 10 races in the 1967 season and 2 of these victories came from "outsiders." Mario Andretti won the Daytona 500 in his Ford, while Parnelli Jones won at Riverside.
International Motorsports Hall of Fame

Richard Petty had a lot to smile about in 1967. With a 426-hemi engine and factory support, he drove his Plymouth to an incredible 27 wins in 48 starts. Cubic inches were up to 426 and 429 in the late 1960s. If NASCAR hadn't reined in the big blocks with restrictor plates and weight penalties, many felt that the motors would have soon been over 500 cubic inches.*International Motorsports Hall of Fame*

While Petty stayed in the "boxy" Plymouth, Buddy Baker campaigned the fastback Charger. Baker ran less than half of the season's races but still managed to win one. *International Motorsports Hall of Fame*

but when the Ford guys began dominating the superspeedways, the Chrysler guys began claiming rules infractions, centering their attention on the Fords' intake manifolds, cylinder heads, and exhaust systems.

As teams were facing stricter rules, there had to be ways to quickly check that they were complying. It was about this time that templates became the standard way for officials to check a car's body profile. Bodies could be modified to make them lower, lighter, and more aerodynamically efficient than the factory bodies.

Early in the season, there were complaints from some teams that the template rules were not being strictly enforced. NASCAR warned teams as they came to Daytona for the Firecracker 400 midway through the season that the rules would be strictly enforced. When the first inspections were conducted at the track, 49 out of 50 cars failed. The garage that day was quite loud with the sound of teams pounding on their car's bodies, trying to pass the template inspection.

Up to the mid-1960s, car builders started with the production-car frame as the backbone, and all of the roll bars were attached to it. In the mid-1960s some began to build the frame and roll cage first and then rebuild the factory sheet metal around it. Holman-Moody is generally given credit for being the first to do this. Others, like Banjo Matthews, soon followed. When building a car in this manner there was a great temptation to modify the final body shape. They would produce a body that still looked stock but that had quite different dimensions than its stock counterpart when carefully measured.

A perfect example of this was Smokey Yunick's way of thinking when building his 1966 Chevelle. The car showed two things. First it showed how intelligent and imaginative Yunick was in his search for speed. It also showed his philosophy of "if there is not a specific rule against something, it must be legal, and if there is a rule against it, then there may be a way to do it without being caught."

Yunick's car had many features not found on stock cars of the time. The front bumper of the car had been widened 2 inches to work as a spoiler. It had fabricated control arms that were adjustable, a vortex generator that was recessed in the car's roofline, and a slick belly pan that dramatically increased the efficiency of the airflow under the car. NASCAR deemed the car very illegal, and it is said that instead of submitting to a full inspection, Yunick got in the car and drove it back to the shop.

When the legal cars were finished on the track in 1967, Mopar and its hemi engine had again dominated the circuit. Plymouth was the big winner, crossing the finish line first 31 times out of 49 starts. Dodge added another 5 victories to give Mopar an impressive 36 wins.

The hottest car on the track was Richard Petty's 1967 Plymouth Satellite. The car had a 426 hemi big block that produced around 600 horsepower. The car had a 115-inch wheelbase and weighed 3,500 pounds. In the front it had a torsion bar suspension and twin shocks. In the rear the car had leaf springs and an 8-3/4-inch differential instead of the standard 9-inch Ford rear end the rest of NASCAR was using.

Richard Petty won the championship in a year in which he would become "the King." In 48 starts he won 27 races and had 38 top-five finishes. Ford followed the Mopar clan, winning 10 times, while Chevrolet managed to win 3 times.

1968

The aerodynamic war really began to heat up in the 1968 season. Ford and Mercury both introduced new models to the track, and both were formidable. Ford's new craft was the Torino, and Mercury fielded the Montego. Both of the cars were fastbacks, and both were fast.

Instead of a nearly vertical rear window, as was the norm for the day, both models had a rear window that sloped from the back of the roof almost to the rear of the deck lid. This gradual slope was much friendlier to the air passing over the car and allowed it to flow, not tumble, off of the roof, a great advantage on the track.

When the cars showed up for the Daytona 500, the fourth race of the 1968 season, Cale Yarborough won the pole with a speed of more than 198 miles per hour. The previous track record was a little over 180, set only one year earlier.

David Pearson and Donnie Allison both drove the new fastback Torino. The car had good aerodynamics (for the times) and had a big 429-cubic-inch powerplant. The Torino moved away from the boxy design of the early and mid-1960s. During the 1960s the racers learned much about making a race car handle. By the late 1960s, aerodynamics was becoming another area of automotive science for them to master. The sloped back of the Torino allowed the air to pass smoothly over the roof and trunk area. On earlier cars, with a near vertical rear window, the air tumbled as it "jumped off of the cliff" at the end of the roof, slowing the car and affecting performance. *International Motorsports Hall of Fame*

75

Cheating

When the rules were established, racers had two choices: obey the rules, or don't. Obeying is pretty straightforward, but the area of not obeying is a little cloudier. A rules infraction will most likely be one of two types.

The first type of rules infraction is the interpretation misunderstanding. Sometimes the rules can be just vague enough for different racers to interpret the same rules in different ways. This brings us to the first law of the NASCAR rule book: The final ruling is given to the opinion of the officials. Typically NASCAR officials will point out this type of infraction out to a team without heavy penalty, as it can be logically argued that the rule in question could be interpreted in another manner.

The second kind of infraction is the premeditated, outright, "We knew we was cheatin'" type. It has always gone on and will continue to go on. Stock car racing has seen gasoline stored in roll cages, nitrous oxide hidden all over the car, weights that fall off of the car, fuel additives, tire-soaking chemicals, and enough illegal parts to sink a ship.

These days there are more officials at the track during a race than there are police directing traffic. And every year, racers pay the price in fines and bad press for trying to sneak one by.

Outright cheating can be performed by fooling the inspectors, or by bypassing the inspectors. Fooling them means the infraction is in the car, but so cleverly hidden that the inspectors will not see it. These can range from undetectable chemicals that improve the tires' grip, to several feet of fuel line encased in the chassis, to parts that should be steel but are, in fact, titanium.

The trick to bypassing the inspectors is to use something illegal but to get it on the car after prerace inspection,

or off of the car before the postrace inspection. David Pearson told me about cars going through inspection with an illegal restrictor plate taped under the fan shroud. After the inspector looked at the legal plate on the car, he would hand it back to a crewmember so that it, and the carburetor, could be replaced. With some slight-of-hand by the crew member, the illegal plate would be fitted to car while the legal plate disappeared into the crew member's shirt.

Because of incidents like this, the inspection procedures grew longer and longer. Every time someone was caught, a new procedure had to be created, and the rule book grew.

One of the best cheating stories of all time centers on the inspection of one of Smokey Yunick's cars at Daytona. I

wasn't there, but I've asked 10 people who ought to know if the story is true, and most say it is. Either way, it's a good yarn.

When Yunick showed up to race, NASCAR called his car in for an inspection. Yunick's car had been getting better mileage than anyone else, so everyone figured he was carrying extra fuel. But when NASCAR disconnected Yunick's fuel tank and removed it from the car for measuring, it was found to be of legal size. NASCAR did find nine other violations, however. When confronted with all of the changes that would have to be made before the car could compete, Yunick decided to drive the car back to his Daytona shop, which was just down the road. He got in the car, fired it up, and drove it away, leaving the disconnected fuel tank at the feet of the NASCAR inspectors!

This car, prepared by Yunick for Gordon Johncock during the 1968 season, spawned one of the most-frequently told rumors in racing history. Legend has it that, after failing a NASCAR inspection that included the removal of the fuel tank, Yunick simply hopped behind the wheel and drove the car away. *John Craft*

Soon the drivers would have another place to run such extreme speeds. In 1968 construction crews broke ground on the next superspeedway, and this one was really super. It was to become the fastest track ever to be run by NASCAR. The site chosen was a piece of land outside of Talladega, Alabama. The site was mostly fields, but part of it had been an airport that was used to train B-17 bomber crews during World War II. At 2.66 miles, it would be the longest oval ever built for stock car racing.

Ford rebounded in 1968 with 20 wins and Mercury added another 7. Dodge won 5 times and Plymouth 16 for a very respectable 21 combined wins for Mopar. General Motors had a lone win with a Chevrolet. David Pearson, driving a Holman-Moody Ford, won another championship with 47 starts, 16 wins, and an incredible 36 top-five finishes.

1969

As the aerodynamic war between Ford and Dodge continued, it produced two of the most memorable cars in the history of the sport. Using the Torino platform, Ford came to race with the Talladega Torino.

The most striking feature of the car was a roofline that so gradually dropped from the back of the roof to the rear of the deck lid that the rear window was more horizontal than vertical. The aerodynamic benefit of this shape was great, especially on the superspeedways, where aerodynamics mean so much.

The slick body shape was accompanied by either a 427 tunnel-port, wedge-head engine or a 429-cubic-inch hemi-headed motor that many say had up to 650 horsepower. The suspension featured twin shocks, adjustable front coil springs, and rear leaf springs.

As the season started, everyone was talking about the Fords and Mercurys. They offered such an edge that even Richard Petty climbed out of his beloved Plymouth and into a Ford. The Torinos and Montegos again looked to be the cars to beat, but later in the year there would be a new Mopar ride that offered much to the driver.

Dodge did not like having relinquished the "most wins" crown to Ford the previous year. Dodge had a great motor, but it was obvious that it was getting whipped in aerodynamics. In 1968 the Dodge people had introduced what they thought was a much more aerodynamic body, but Ford had smoked them on the track.

While the body was slicker, there were a few problems, one of which was a relatively large grille, which created a great deal of drag. The engineers went back to the drawing board and made changes that resulted in one of the coolest race (and street) cars ever to come out of Detroit: the Dodge Daytona.

The biggest changes were the addition of a nose clip and a rear wing. The nose clip was extremely efficient at cutting through the air and was designed so that the top of the clip created downforce as the air passed over it. The faster the car went, the more the downforce, and the better

the car handled. To balance the downforce effect, engineers mounted a high-rise wing on the back of the car. The angle of the wing could be changed to adjust the downforce.

Plymouth soon followed Dodge with the Plymouth Superbird. It was a Belvedere body with the new front clip and rear wing. The introduction of these new cars brought Richard Petty back to Plymouth. While the Fords still won more races in the 1969 season, Dodges did well late in the year.

The downforce these cars generated gave them a tendency to put too much pressure on the tires, causing them to shred and blow. All of this was happening as the new Talladega Superspeedway was opening, and it was part of the reason for the driver boycott that took place at that track's first event.

During the season there was a movement by the drivers to unite and form an association in order to better their

The Dodge Daytona was like no other car. Although greater effort would be put into aerodynamics in the 1990s, the Daytona is perhaps the most visual example of NASCAR racing's aerodynamic obsession. During a boycott by the top drivers, Richard Brickhouse won his only Grand National race in the inaugural Talladega event. *International Motorsports Hall of Fame*

competitive position in the political arena of the sport. Richard Petty led the movement, and the fruit of his labors was the PDA, or Professional Drivers Association. Basically, the drivers wanted more driver and crew conveniences, a pension plan, and insurance.

Petty was elected president with Cale Yarborough and Elmo Langley as vice presidents. The board of directors included Bobby Allison, Donnie Allison, Lee Roy Yarbrough, Charlie Glotzbach, Pete Hamilton, Buddy Baker, James Hylton, and David Pearson.

The stage was set for a battle of the wills between the drivers and Big Bill France, and the new Talladega track would be the battlefield. The track was completed in 1969 and the first race was scheduled for September 14. Before the race there was a tire-testing session at the new track, and the results were not good.

The major complaints were that the track was too rough and that the tires would not hold up. In an effort to squelch the complaints, France, who was 59 years old at the time, drove the track at 175 miles per hour in a Holman-Moody Ford. France even entered the Talladega race, hoping that if he competed he would be allowed to join the PDA.

As the teams showed up for the Talladega race and began to run laps, sure enough, there were tire problems.

The speeds and the terrific downforce created by the cars, especially the new Dodge Daytonas, were causing tire failure after tire failure. The problems were so severe that Firestone pulled up its stakes and left. The PDA's position was that the race should be postponed so that better tires could be developed.

France wanted the show to go on and the rhetoric got more and more harsh. France's position was that if the tires were blowing while running at 190 miles per hour, then the drivers should slow down.

The drivers did not share his opinion, and 32 of them left the track and went home. Only 13 of the Grand National drivers stayed to run the race. France went to the Grand Touring ranks to fill out the field, and when the green flag dropped there were the 13 Grand National drivers plus 36 Grand Touring drivers. Richard Brickhouse won the event, scoring his one and only Grand National win. By the next race the season got back on track and all of the drivers were back competing.

General Motors' lack of support for the sport once again bought it a big goose egg in the win column at the end of the year. Ford won 26 times and Mercury won 4 times to make the fastback Ford products the biggest winners. Plymouth dropped to 2 wins, but Dodge came through with 22 wins with the new aero Daytona.

The solution to the Charger's aerodynamic deficiency relative to the Torino was the "Daytona" option. The Daytona model of the Charger was a special option available for both street drivers and NASCAR racers. The car did a good job answering the challenge of the aerodynamic Ford fastbacks. Here, a crew member checks the condition of the left front tire as his teammates change the right side tires. The big Dodges had so much power and downforce that overheating and blistering the tires could be a problem. *International Motorsports Hall of Fame*

David Pearson won his third championship driving the Holman-Moody Ford. He ran in 51 of the season's 54 races, racking up 11 wins and a healthy 42 top-five finishes.

As the 1960s came to an end, the sport was becoming more popular with fans, the press, and auto manufacturers. The factories were making more and more performance-oriented options aimed at NASCAR and a public that could buy cheap gas. Constant changes to the cars' engines and bodies, however, were making it very difficult for NASCAR to balance the competition.

NASCAR knew if one manufacturer dominated, the support from the other manufacturers, and the fans, would leave the sport. Purists felt that if a manufacturer made a better product, it should win (usually these purists were the guys who had the hot model—when the competition came out with something better they usually relinquished their purist status).

But France knew that NASCAR was a "show." It was entertainment. The race had to be won on the track and not in the engineering departments of the factories. Controlling this environment would be one of the biggest challenges as the sport entered the 1970s. Others would include driver boycotts, a fuel crisis, and fading factory support.

The 1970s saw great change in the stock cars that ran the NASCAR circuit. Engine sizes would drop, the car bodies would become more aerodynamic, and sponsors would become more and more important. *International Motorsports Hall of Fame*

Chapter Four

The 1970s

As the 1970 season got under way, France was still smarting from his run-in with the Professional Drivers Association at Talladega. The conflict between the organization and France was far from over. France felt that the organization was a threat to his leadership of NASCAR. After the episode at Talladega, the big issue for France was making sure that the show would go on. The drivers left France high and dry after building a track, promoting the race, and selling tickets to the fans. When the drivers walked out a day before the event, it had left him in a very tenuous position. To help ensure that this would never happen again, a new clause was added to the entry blank for each race.

It was a good faith clause, basically stating that by entering the race, the owner of the car was guaranteeing that the car would run the race. Even if the driver backed out, a substitute would be put in the car. The clause was so far-reaching that it ultimately gave NASCAR the right to put a driver in the car if the owner couldn't or wouldn't.

The owners did not like the rule. In a way, it put the control of their equipment in NASCAR's hands. But the factories were pushing to go racing and the drivers wanted to race, so everyone finally signed the forms and went racing. France had his guaranteed show and the power meter swung away from the PDA and back in France's direction.

The root cause of the Talladega boycott was still there, however. Buddy Baker tested at Talladega on March 24, 1970, and consistently turned laps around the 200-mile-per-hour mark. But the tires continued to be a problem. At the first Talladega race in 1970, Goodyear introduced a new treadless tire that still blistered and failed under the extreme heat and pressure.

This time boycotts were not necessary. Instead, NASCAR made a rule change to require a 1-1/4-inch restrictor plate on all of the cars. This plate would choke down the air and fuel flow to the engine. As the carburetors had a 1-11/16 inch opening to start with, the plates had a pretty big effect. On average it slowed the cars down about 13 miles per hour at Talladega, and this was enough to appease the drivers. This time they would race at Talladega.

And the drivers would be getting more exposure while racing. ABC signed a deal with NASCAR in December 1969 to televise nine races in 1970. Five of the broadcasts would be live. The only problem was that ABC's *Wide World of Sports* was only 1-1/4 hours long and a race usually lasted about 4 hours. The solution was to show taped highlights of the beginning of the race and go broadcast live only during the last 30 minutes of the race.

The factories continued to be fickle and success did not mean continuation. At the end of the year, Chrysler announced that it would again cut back factory support, moving from six factory-backed teams to two. It would still support Petty Enterprises, with Richard Petty driving a Plymouth Superbird and Buddy Baker in a Dodge Daytona. Bobby Isaac and Bobby Allison, who both drove Dodges, would not receive factory support. Despite this, Isaac would win the 1970 Grand National Championship and Allison would finish second. Isaac had 22 wins in 47 starts with 32 top-five finishes. Allison had 3 wins in 46 starts with 30 top-fives.

Mopar ruled the 1970 season in a big way. Dodge had 17 wins and Plymouth had 21. Bobby Isaac had his 11 wins in his Dodge, and Richard Petty led the way for Plymouth with 18. Ford managed to visit victory lane 6 times and Mercury 4 to keep the Ford products from being totally embarrassed. General Motors went winless with all four of its production divisions.

1971

A new NASCAR era was born in the early 1970s when NASCAR and R. J. Reynolds completed the biggest sponsorship deal ever to be attempted in stock car racing. Bill France, always selling the promotional side of stock car racing, convinced R. J. Reynolds to sponsor the entire series.

This was uncharted territory. Sponsors had backed single events or cars but never the entire series. If money was to be made having companies sponsor single events, then logic would dictate that sponsorship of a whole slate of events would be even better.

But having a single entity supporting the entire series forced new thinking. It was such a large business deal that those in charge (at this point Bill France and R. J. Reynolds) had to look at the condition of the sport as a whole and thoroughly evaluate what was working and what was not.

It was clear from the beginning that this new partnership would mean changes. First to go were the events under 250 miles. This, in essence, eliminated many of the smaller venues. The season would also be scaled down to 31 races. It was felt that fewer "big events" would be better than many smaller events. The 31-race season would also help all of the teams run every event. With the staggering number of events in the previous seasons, many of the top teams still did not run all of the races.

The 1970 season saw the winged Dodges continue to win. Here, Bobby Allison takes the white flag on his way to winning the Atlanta 500 in Mario Rossi's Dodge Daytona. *International Motorsports Hall of Fame*

During this period, sponsorship became more important to the individual teams. Factory support was again on the decline, as was the entire American automotive industry.

A large part of Richard Petty's success can be attributed to his relationship with STP. In 1972, STP hooked up with Petty Enterprises to promote its new oil filter. With Plymouth scaling down its support, it gave Petty the money to still compete. R. J. Reynolds' involvement and commitment to the sport, plus the television coverage (though still limited), made it a little easier for the teams to find sponsors.

Part of the R. J. Reynolds deal stipulated that the Grand National name for NASCAR's top series would be changed to the Winston Cup Grand National Series. Winston would begin its commitment by putting $100,000 into the pot for the season championship—a great incentive for the teams to run all of the races.

Winston also put an admirable effort into promoting each event. Large advertisements were placed in newspapers and magazines. Billboards were erected to promote events on a local level. This promotion brought more interest, and more interest meant that more sponsors would want to come into the sport.

In 1971 General Motors managed to get back to victory lane 3 times with Chevrolet. Tiny Lund scored 2 of these wins driving a Camaro. Ford had 4 wins and Mercury 11. Bobby Allison won 7 races in a Mercury, 2 in a Dodge, and 2 in a Ford (1 of which was a win in Winston-Salem on a quarter-mile paved track, where Allison drove a Mustang) for a total of 11 wins.

But the winged Plymouth was again the car to beat in 1971. Plymouth had 22 total wins, with 21 of those courtesy of Richard Petty. The only other Plymouth win was by Pete

The Dodge Charger was not just about horsepower—it was also about downforce. The front fascia and hood helped the air push the front of the car down, and the high wing (which was adjustable) did the same for the rear. *International Motorsports Hall of Fame*

Hamilton in a 125-mile qualifying race for the Daytona 500. Dodge tacked on another 8 wins, giving the Mopar camp a total of 30 victories.

1972

Nineteen seventy-two began what has become known as the "modern era" of NASCAR. It is the point at which the sport moved from about 50 races a year to about 30 and at which a new points system was started. Now the winner of an event got 100 points, second place got 98 points, third place received 96, and so on. Points were also to be awarded for laps completed. These lap points would vary depending on the length of the track being run. The breakdown was as follows:

Tracks under 1 mile	.25 point per lap
1-mile tracks	.50 point per lap
1.3-mile tracks (Darlington)	.70 point per lap
1.5-mile tracks	.75 point per lap
2-mile tracks	1.00 point per lap
Tracks over 2.5 miles	1.25 points per lap

The points system was designed not only to reward the winner of the event, but also to motivate teams to run as many laps as possible in order to accumulate points.

The cars looked a bit different when the season started. The winged Mopars were gone, a victim of tightening rules. The special engine rules that applied to the aero cars had caused their demise. They were replaced by the "Coke bottle"

There was no telling what Bobby Allison would show up in during the 1970s. Here, his Mustang is filled up by a colorfully clothed fuel can man on the way to victory in a 250-lap event on the quarter-mile paved track in Winston-Salem, North Carolina. *International Motorsports Hall of Fame*

The primary reason for the demise of the winged cars was a rule that required any car with a special aerodynamic package to run a smaller engine. As a result, the wingless Dodge appeared in 1972. The new Charger was a much less radical design than its predecessor, but it was still a very successful racing platform. The car began with a 426 hemi, but because the hemis were restricted by the rules, many Dodge teams switched back to the 426 with the conventional wedge heads. While the two engines had the same displacement, the wedge-heads were not hammered by the NASCAR rule book.
International Motorsports Hall of Fame

The new Charger weighed in at 3,800 pounds and featured ventilated drum brakes, a torsion-bar front suspension, leaf springs in the rear, and two shocks per wheel. Here, Buddy Baker trails A. J. Foyt in his Wood Brothers Mercury. Baker would eventually pass Foyt to finish second, demoting Foyt to third.
International Motorsports Hall of Fame

Dodge, a departure from the old body, which proved to be a very strong competitor. The winged car's replacement, while a less radical design, was still very successful.

The new Charger would come to be a favorite of Richard Petty. It had a very long production run and this, coupled with NASCAR's rules allowing older models to compete, meant that the car would run from 1972 to 1978. It began with the powerful 426 hemi under the hood, but as that motor configuration was being hammered harder and harder by the rules, the team switched to the 426 with the conventional wedge heads.

The 1972 Charger weighed 3,800 pounds and had a wheelbase of 118 inches. The suspension still featured adjustable torsion bars, beefed-up A-frames, leaf springs, floating hubs, twin shocks on all four wheels, and ventilated drum brakes.

Richard Petty won his fourth championship with the Charger in 1972. Throughout the year, Petty battled Bobby Allison, who finished a close second driving a Chevrolet. Petty ended the championship with 8,701.4 points and 8 wins in 31 starts. Allison had 10 wins in 31 races, but finished with only 8,573.5 points.

But, if the championship had been decided based on winning percentage, David Pearson would have won in the Wood Brothers' 1971 Mercury Cyclone. He took 6 wins in only 17 starts, with 12 top-5 finishes, and 13 top-10 finishes.

Once again the tide of factory support was ebbing. The new big-block hemis were being restricted, so the Wood Brothers went back to the 1967 version of the 427, which was allowed to run with a bigger restrictor plate.

The manufacturers stacked up pretty evenly in 1972. Chevrolet had 10 wins, Mercury 9, Dodge 4, and Plymouth 8. Mopar edged out the others with 12 combined wins.

Perhaps the biggest news of the entire 1972 season was when Bill France Sr. handed over the reins of the sport to

Bill France Jr. Big Bill would still be around and would be the sport's ultimate voice, but the day-to-day grind of running the sport was now in the hands of his son.

1973

Bill France Jr. would not have to wait long for political activity in his new job, as NASCAR won another victory in 1973. The Frances had never wanted to deal with unionized drivers, but they had been forced to for the last few years. But in 1973, Richard Petty resigned from the Professional Drivers Association, an entity that he had helped form a scant four years earlier. His defection pretty much took the wind out of the organization's sails.

On the track, the big blocks were still king and the results proved it. However, other manufacturers were tiring of the constant success of the large-displacement motors, and one of the most exhausted was the Chevrolet camp. In addition, many owners and drivers felt that there were many cars running that were far from legal. It seemed that more and more drivers were either cheating or were convinced someone else was.

It came to a head at Charlotte. Bobby Allison, one of the most talented drivers and mechanics to ever touch a race car, was running as well as he ever had, but with only limited success. At Charlotte he had proclaimed before the race that he would protest any car that finished ahead of him. Allison appeared to have a point when pole sitter Charlie Glotzbach was stripped of his starting position after his car was found to have an illegal restrictor plate. The plate had been rigged so that it could be pulled out of the way by the driver via a small cable. In other words, it wasn't a matter of an accident in manufacturing by the team. Rather, it was a case of pure, premeditated hooking. After requalifying with a legal restrictor plate, Glotzbach started 36th.

Allison knew that for every guy who was caught there were many who weren't. Cale Yarborough won the race in Junior Johnson's famous No. 11 Chevrolet. Richard Petty finished second in his mighty Dodge. Allison followed them in third place in his No. 12 Chevrolet.

After the race all three of the cars were to be inspected. Allison's car was quickly declared legal but no word came from the inspection area on either Yarborough's Chevrolet or Richard's Dodge. Everyone waited and waited. And waited.

Finally, six hours after the race was over, the officials announced that the results of the engine measurements would be sent to NASCAR headquarters and they would make the final announcement. Obviously, the people at the track did not want to decide how to handle this mess and had decided to leave it up to the folks at headquarters.

Again, everyone waited and waited. Some did not wait for the results to complain. Richard Howard, who promoted the race and happened to own the car that won, fired the first shot when he stated that if the results of the race were changed he would sue and let the court decide the issue.

The ruling that finally rumbled forth from NASCAR stated that the results of the race would stand, but not because the three cars were legal. Instead, their reasoning was that the inspection procedures used before the race were inadequate. In other words, there had some cheatin' going on, but no one would be penalized.

Allison was livid. Now it was his turn to contemplate using the courts. First he withdrew from the next race. Then he assembled the media and announced that if the strict rules of competition had been applied to all competitors, then he would have won the race. He would have collected first-place money instead of third-place money, and he would have accumulated more championship points, which would have meant more money at the end of the year. As a result, he was suing NASCAR.

During all of this, Bill France Jr. had remained silent (good move). But things were quickly getting out of hand. Allison agreed to meet France in Atlanta to discuss the situation.

Bobby Allison would be one of the main catalysts of change in the sport. His protest in 1973 helped legitimize the integrity of NASCAR's inspection process. *International Motorsports Hall of Fame*

After a long session both sides came out with the highest respect for each other. It was announced that Allison would race in the next event and that NASCAR would work very hard to make sure that none of these "misunderstandings" would happen in the future. NASCAR also announced that there would now be a postrace inspection of the carburetor plate, air cleaner, and engine size.

No one ever revealed the details of the meeting, but it was obvious that Allison had won this battle. His only comment to the press was, "I have received satisfactory restitution, and you can read that anyway you want to." It is believed that France made some compensation to Allison, which kept him racing. Bill Jr., just like his

father, could bend when necessary to provide for the future of NASCAR.

Benny Parsons won the 1973 Championship with 1 victory in 28 starts. Cale Yarborough finished second in the points with 4 wins. Richard Petty fought adversity throughout the year. He had 6 wins but could only manage fifth place in the championship race.

Once again the winningest driver by percentage was David Pearson. Pearson continued to run a limited schedule, racing only 18 times in 1973. But in those 18 starts he had 11 wins and 14 top-five finishes.

Ford again went winless in 1973, but Mercury won 11 times, and David Pearson and the Wood Brothers were

Because the Charger had a long production run, and because NASCAR allowed older cars to continue to race, the "Coke bottle" Dodge would win races from 1972 to 1977.
International Motorsports Hall of Fame

responsible for all of those. Chevrolet dropped from 10 wins the previous year to 7 in 1973. Dodge ended the year with 8 wins and Plymouth added another 1. Mark Donohue won a race for AMC when he outpaced the field at Riverside in his Matador.

As the season came to a close, events halfway around the world would again threaten the future of the sport. A bunch of guys in the Middle East decided that Europe, the United States, and the rest of the free world were not paying enough for the crude oil they were buying. The result for NASCAR was that it would soon be viewed as a sport that did nothing but waste precious fuel.

The writing was on the wall for the big blocks. It has always been said that when building power there is no substitute for cubic inches, and the big blocks certainly offered a lot of cubic inches. But there were two reasons for teams wanting to get away from big blocks. First, if they ran one, they knew that it would be with a restrictor plate. Second, even if they could get more speed out of the choked-down motor, they would most likely be rewarded with a smaller restrictor plate.

The early 1970s saw a return to relative parity between the big three automakers. Here David Pearson, in a Ford, passes Dick Brook's Dodge on the way to victory at Bristol in 1971.
International Motorsports Hall of Fame

continued on page 95

91

The Engine

With 750 horsepower under each hood, the command to start engines unleashes 32,250 horses to run around the track. I've spent a little time around horses, and that's a lot of dang horses. They rumble during the pace laps and they scream when the green flag drops. As far as sound goes, the first lap is the best. You're not used to it yet and it always sounds loudest on the first lap. The particular effects of the sound vary, depending on which track you are at. There's nothing like the rumble of the cars as they race together in a pack on a superspeedway. But then again there's nothing like the sound of the acceleration at a short track.

In the pits at Bristol, the cars are so loud that without ear protection the sound just turns into a white noise, like static coming through Led Zeppelin's PA system.

On the Winston Cup circuit, victory is usually a matter of handling, but horsepower never hurts. Drivers love to be able to power past other cars on the straightaway, which they can more easily do if they have more engine power than the other guy. With the strict rules in place and the tendency for engine builders to change teams, the horsepower war is surprisingly equal today between the top teams.

Each engine begins life as a raw block. Only small-block V-8s are allowed. While there are many small blocks out there, with many different configurations and displacements, the NASCAR rules allow Ford the 351-cubic-inch block and General Motors the 350-cubic-inch. The maximum compression allowed is 12:1 in any cylinder.

In the 1950s most engines used stock components. Later, special parts were offered by the factories to increase

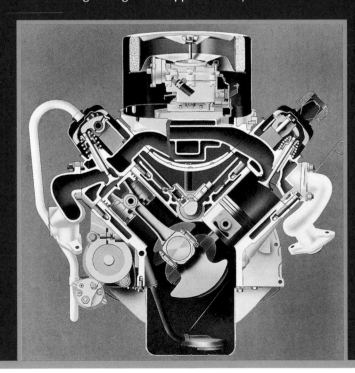

The race for power heated up in the 1960s during the factory horsepower wars. The quickest way to increase power was to increase the engine's displacement. While the Hudson Hornet had been successful during the 1950s with a 303-cubic-inch straight-six, a decade later the design to beat was a V-8 displacing more than 400 cubic inches. Dodge ran a 426-cubic-inch powerplant, Chevy had the 427, and Ford had both the 427 and the 429

In order to slow the power race, NASCAR began to penalize the big blocks (especially the hemis) with restrictor plates and extra weight penalties. The result was a migration to the small blocks, like the engine shown here. Displacement settled out at 358 cubic inches. Early small blocks generated around 500 horsepower. With the high-quality parts available to racers, and the vast acquired knowledge of how to tweak horsepower out of an engine, today's small blocks generate close to 800 horsepower. Just imagine what one of today's engine builders could do with a 426 hemi.

the performance of the stock engines. Since they were offered to the general public, they were legal to race on Sunday.

In the 1960s the horsepower wars became much more intense. The manufacturers, especially Ford and Chrysler, upped the ante each year, developing bigger and more powerful engines.

The primary way the factories gained horsepower was by increasing displacement. But as the cubic inches grew, so did the rules restricting them. The engines were putting out more power than the suspensions and bodies of the time could handle. NASCAR began by limiting cubic inches. Then it resorted to restrictor plates.

One of the biggest problems for NASCAR was that if one manufacturer became too dominant, the fans would not like it. So the rules became an attempt to balance the field.

As the big blocks became more and more restricted, there was a move to the small block in the 1970s. As the Detroit divisions homogenized their lines, engine models for the independent models disappeared. For instance, Buicks, Chevrolets, Oldsmobiles, and Pontiacs could all run a Chevrolet engine.

In the 1980s and 1990s the small blocks became more and more refined. At times NASCAR would step in when the search for horsepower got out of hand. For example, the techniques used in building cylinder heads were becoming both exotic and expensive. Teams were doing so many modifications that the expense was getting out of hand. A team could easily have $20,000 to $30,000 invested in a set of heads.

So NASCAR specified a short list of allowable cylinder heads and put specific limits on the amount of things that

Winston Cup engine speeds have increased to the point where turning over 9,000 rpm is common. Harmonic problems at a particular rpm level cause many valvetrain problems. If the engine runs at the rpm level where bad harmonics occur, this will increase the chances of engine failure. This is especially a problem at longer tracks where engines run for a long time in one rpm range.

Engine builders try to design the engine so that the bad harmonics occur within an rpm range that is not sustained. As the engine accelerates or decelerates through the bad range, harmonics are usually not a problem.

When building so much horsepower and

Modern teams will bring a half dozen engines to a race. There is the practice engine, the qualifying engine, the race engine, and a few back-up engines, just in case. Here, a qualifying engine is pulled from the car, to be replaced with a practice motor.

could be changed. But even with all of the rules, today's engine builders can get around 800 horsepower out of an old-style solid-lifter carbureted engine.

There are now three motors running in Winston Cup racing. The racing divisions of Dodge, Ford, and General Motors manufacture the cast-iron blocks (aluminum blocks aren't allowed), which are made specifically for racing and do not appear in any production vehicle. A car's engine must correspond to its make, meaning you can't put a Ford engine in a Chevrolet body.

Today's search for horsepower comes in small increments. There aren't any 10- or 20-horsepower improvements left. Now it is a matter of a half a horsepower here and another half there. Engine builders piece together enough of these half-horsepower tricks to gain an advantage on the track, or, at worst, to keep up with the competition.

turning so many rpm, engine cooling becomes a difficult issue. Winston Cup cars have a regular cooling system (radiator and water pump), but they also use increased oil flow to keep the engine cool. Cup cars run a "dry sump" oil system, which is not commonly found on production vehicles.

Instead of the oil flowing down to the pan to be recycled through the engine by a pump located at the bottom of the oil pan, the dry-sump system keeps the oil in motion at all times. The pump is mounted on the outside of the engine (much the same as an alternator is mounted) and is driven by a belt. After the oil runs through the engine, it is quickly "picked up" from the bottom of the oil pan and pumped back into the oil system. During circulation the oil passes through many feet of hose, an oil tank mounted in the left rear of the car, and an oil cooler mounted in the left front of the car. Proper cooling is essential to be competitive on the track.

In 1973 the sport once again saw a challenge from a brand other than the big three. Since 1955, no makes outside General Motors, Ford, or Chrysler had won a race. But in 1973 AMC stunned the racing world by entering NASCAR competition (the car was prepared by Roger Penske) and quickly winning a race. Their first win came at the Riverside road course with Mark Donohue at the wheel. *International Motorsports Hall of Fame*

Continued from page 91

The restrictor plate rules were changing rapidly, and each time it meant that the teams would have to go back to the drawing boards with their engines. As a result of this, Petty Engineering began to look to the small block in the mid-1970s, and spent more than $50,000 in 1974 learning to build power with fewer (only 358) cubic inches.

But a Ford ran the first successful small block. In 1973 Bud Moore fielded a 358-cubic-inch small block engine housed in a Ford Torino. Moore had some experience with small blocks from his Trams Am days. He started with a 351 Cleveland, came up with his own induction system, and beefed up the entire engine. The resulting engine was rated at around 500 horsepower—plenty to run with the choked-down big blocks. His effort would provide the blueprint for the future of Winston Cup engines.

Moore's car did well. It finished second in the 1973 Daytona 500 with Bobby Isaac at the wheel. It again ran well at Talladega until lap 90, when Isaac pitted and retired from the sport on the spot. The next driver to drive the car was a brash newcomer named Darrell Waltrip.

While the Plymouths and Dodges dominated the 1970s, the toughest guy to beat was still David Pearson, and he still drove a Mercury. Pearson first drove a Wood

The big blocks were becoming a thing of the past. Engine power was growing faster than any other area of performance. Restrictor plates were the most common method of limiting horsepower. These rules more or less forced the teams to move back to the small blocks. Even though they had less displacement, the lack of restrictions allowed them to make more horsepower. *International Motorsports Hall of Fame*

Stock cars were again threatened with extinction in the mid-1970s. With a fuel crisis sweeping the country, many saw the Sunday races as a waste of fuel. NASCAR voluntarily limited practice and shortened races as a goodwill gesture. It worked, and the cars raced on. *International Motorsports Hall of Fame*

Brothers Cyclone and then a Montego. They ran a limited schedule through most of his career but still managed to win three championships. Pearson and the Wood Brothers ran 143 races, won 43 of them, and put the car on the pole 51 times.

As the 1970s got under way the big blocks were an endangered species. Here Lee Roy Yarbrough tunes his Dodge's big motor before heading onto the track. In 1973 Bud Moore switched to the 358-cubic inch small-block Ford engine to power his Torino. His experience building small blocks in the Trans Am series helped Bud produce around 500 horsepower with his Cleveland engine. Moore's small-block Torino won the 1973 Daytona 500, proving that the small blocks could win on the big tracks. *International Motorsports Hall of Fame*

1974

In 1974 nonracing factors once again threatened the sport. More than 90 million gallons of gasoline were consumed in auto racing each year in the United States. While this was a drop in the bucket compared to the entire nation's fuel consumption, it was a way for sensationalists to get some headlines. Keep in mind that in the first 20 or so years of NASCAR's existence, there had been serious movements to get rid of auto racing. The Detroit automakers had at times fully embraced stock car racing and at other times had completely ignored it. Bill France Jr. and Sr. would both move quickly to fight this new threat.

Federal energy officials were looking for ways to save gasoline everywhere. All forms of auto racing were nervous. In November 1973, leaders of NASCAR, USAC, IMSA, and the NHRA met in Chicago to figure out what to do. The Frances saw regulation coming and took a very active position. They voluntarily cut the race distances at their tracks by 10 percent (for the first 15 races of the season), and asked all other track owners on the circuit to do the same. In many races the number of cars in the field was also lowered. They cut practice time and limited the amount of fuel that the teams could use during practice. As a result of their actions, they cut the fuel usage by about 30 percent. This was not only enough for Department of Energy to forget about regulations—it even praised auto racing for their voluntary assistance.

Once again in 1974, NASCAR changed the point system. The new one was as bad as the previous

By the mid-1970s the teams would be poring over small blocks instead of big blocks. It would take a while, but the engine builders would eventually get more than two horsepower per cubic inch, without resorting to such modern conveniences as turbochargers and fuel injection. *International Motorsports Hall of Fame*

Richard Petty had 10 wins for Dodge in 1974. Here he straps in for a race. By the mid-1970s, the roll cage had more bars to provide better protection for the driver. *International Motorsports Hall of Fame*

system (probably worse), and now linked points to the amount of money won. The race winnings (special award money did not count) were multiplied by the number of races started, and then divided by 1,000. It was a bad system and it would not last.

The big block versus small block battle was also coming to a head. If you think that modern-day rules changes are bad, they were a lot worse during the early 1970s.

NASCAR always has tried to level the playing field between the manufacturers. Some automakers, when losing consistently, might go to the trouble to reengineer and come up with something new, but they might just pull out of the sport. Fans as well would tire of one winner and the entire series would fail. The drivers and team owners didn't help the situation either. If they were on the winning side they would say they are just doing their job and the other teams should work harder. The losing teams said that the rules favor the winning guys and unless they got help, they might as well quit.

A lot of this attitude could be traced to the restrictor plates that were mandatory on the big-block cars. The Mopar hemis had been hit hard, and their guys were mad. They had a great car and a great motor and because they were so good, they were getting hammered by the rules.

From a car owner's point of view, the common denominator for any rules change was expense. In 1974 it seemed as soon as they prepared cars to race, the rules would be changed and the owner had to foot the bill to reconfigure the cars. NASCAR had been more or less prepared to change the rules before the 1974 season began, but the fuel crisis had taken a lot of their energy, so the season started with the same rules as 1973.

The first major rule change was the elimination of the restrictor plate on the large-displacement motors. Instead of a restrictor plate, any engine over 366 cubic inches would have to run a "rules approved" Holley carburetor. This new rule further decreased the power of the big blocks and was popular with the small-block guys.

The first race after the rules change was

the Atlanta 500. Richard Petty and Cale Yarborough stuck with the small blocks but were noticeably off of the pace. As a result there was another rules change, which gave a little air back to the big-block guys, but the help was minimal. More and more teams were switching to the small blocks.

A third rules change brought two new carburetors for the big block. The size of the track being run determined which one was used.

Another announcement was the proclamation that, as of June 24, the maximum displacement for the small blocks would be dropped from 366 cubic inches to 358 cubic inches.

At the time of this writing in 2001, 358 cubic inches is still the maximum displacement allowed.

The fifth major rules change for 1974 limited the modifications that the Ford teams were making to cylinder heads. The sum of all of these rules was that the writing was on the wall for the big blocks. Regardless of the make they were running, or the size engine they were running, all of the teams were sick of rules changes by the end of 1974.

As far as the competition went in 1974, three drivers won 27 of the 30 races. Richard Petty and Cale Yarborough both won 10 races in 30 starts. David Pearson,

once again running a limited schedule, won 7 races in only 19 starts. The only other winners that year were Bobby Allison, who had 2 wins, and Earl Ross, who had 1. Richard Petty's performance was the most consistent, and it won him his fifth championship.

Chevrolet led the way in 1974 with a dozen wins, thanks mainly to Cale Yarborough, who had 10 wins in his Chevy. Mercury's 7 wins all came with David Pearson behind the wheel. Dodge had 10 wins, with Richard Petty winning all of them. AMC got credit for Bobby Allison's 1 victory.

1975

NASCAR abandoned the one-year-old, money-based points system and once again adopted a new system. This time NASCAR got it right, and the new system survives to this day. The winner of each race receives 175 points. Decending from 2nd through 6th place, each driver receives 5 points less than the previous driver. For example, 2nd place receives 170 points, 3rd 165, etc. Seventh through 11th place have 4-point differentials, and 12th to 43rd have a 3-point differential between each place. The 43rd-place car receives 34 points. Five bonus points are given to any driver who leads a lap, and five are given to the driver who leads the most laps.

The media's interest in the sport also continued to grow. In 1974 ABC televised the last half of the Daytona 500. In 1975 it expanded its coverage and televised the second halves of the Daytona 500 and the Atlanta 500. It would

also show, on a delayed broadcast, races from Dover (the Mason-Dixon 500), Darlington (the Southern 500), Charlotte (National 500), and another at Daytona (the Firecracker 500). The Daytona 500 was broadcast at the same time as an NBA game and an NHL game, but the race had far more viewers than either of the other two events.

After AMC's initial success, Bobby Allison jumped on board. He first drove Penske-prepared Matadors, but later built his own in his Hueytown, Alabama, shop. Allison won once in the car in 1974 and three times in 1975. Bobby Allison often did much of his own engineering and is arguably the greatest stock car racer to ever live. While others drivers may have more impressive statistics, none can match his record of a great driving record plus numerous mechanical innovations.

Allison came up with many concepts still used in Winston Cup cars. His contribution to design included the front steer suspension arrangement and brake fluid recirculation. One of the best stories about Bobby came from early in his career. He needed a new motor the night before a race. Allison didn't have a spare, so he found a junkyard and purchased a used school bus engine (school bus engines had four-bolt mains) and rebuilt it in his hotel room the night before the race. After checking out (leaving the maid a nice surprise) he proceeded to the track, where he won the race.
International Motorsports Hall of Fame

It would turn out to be an important time for the sport. Television would be a key link in the money flow to the financially struggling owners. If a race was not televised, the event would only reach the people at the track and through a few lines of print in the write-ups in the Monday paper. If a sponsor's car ran well during a televised race, it could reach millions of people for extended periods of time and, it was hoped, would have the company's name called a few times by the announcers.

The entry of television into the sport was the primary factor that shaped it into what it is today. Television meant exposure that NASCAR could use to demand greater sums for sponsorship. Television allowed the really big money to begin flowing to the teams and drivers.

But there were new problems in 1975. The country's economy was not good and money was tight with everyone. When the factories backed out once again, there were no cheap (or free) parts floating around. Costs were up.

Well-established, successful teams such as Holman-Moody, Banjo Matthews, Cotton Owens, and Ray Nichols folded shop. Junior Johnson was only able to keep his Chevrolets running with a last-minute deal. Johnson and Yarborough had won 10 races in 1974 and 4 in 1973. This shows how even the top teams with top drivers had financial worries. RC Cola came on board and bailed out on the Bud Moore team and driver Buddy Baker.

Because money was so tight, NASCAR introduced another new system. In 1975 the Awards and Achievement plan paid four teams what was, in essence, appearance money. Petty Enterprises with Richard Petty driving, K&K Insurance with Dave Marcis driving, Junior Johnson with Cale Yarborough driving, and Bud Moore with Buddy Baker driving, were each paid $3,000 for each superspeedway race and $2,000 for each short-track race run.

This helped the top teams concentrate more on racing and less on financing. It also assured France that the top drivers would be on the track every Sunday afternoon. NASCAR would also pay all independent teams in the top 20 in points $500 for each superspeedway race, and $250 for each short-track race.

Dodge led the way in 1975 with 14 wins. Thirteen of these came from Petty, with Dave Marcis being the only other driver to win in a Dodge. Buddy Baker got Ford back into victory lane with 4 wins. Mercury won 3 times, with David Pearson again behind the wheel for each victory. Yarborough, Parsons, and Waltrip combined to give Chevrolet 6 wins. The AMC-Bobby Allison combination came on strong with 3 wins.

1976

Nineteen seventy-six would see new drivers emerge. Two years earlier, Darrell Waltrip had driven in 16 races and had led 15 of them. He and his wife, Stevie, fielded a home-grown effort that showed Darrell's potential. In 1976 the man who would become the sports third-winningest driver (tied with Bobby Allison at 84 wins) would drive for the DiGard team and would land Gatorade as a sponsor. It wouldn't take long for Waltrip to become one of the sport's most outspoken personalities.

At the Daytona 500, A. J. Foyt, Dave Marcis, and Darrell Waltrip would all have their qualifying speeds thrown out. For Marcis, the reason was fuel pressure assist devices, or nitrous oxide. For Foyt and Waltrip, the reason was blocking off too much of the radiator, which improved aerodynamics. Waltrip quickly voiced his opinion. "If you don't cheat you look like an idiot. If you do it and don't get caught you look like a hero. If you do it and get caught you look like a dope. Put me in the category where I belong."

The media's NASCAR articles began to focus more and more on cheating. One of the favorite methods of the time was the use of nitrous oxide.

Nitrous oxide is a gas that for years had been used by both dentists and racers. When given to a human it reduces pain and improves attitude, which is where it got its other name, "laughing gas." When it is administered to an internal combustion

Darrell Waltrip became a force in the 1970s. Darrell was young and often had a bit of an attitude, both on and off of the track. His competitive nature and great driving skill would result in 84 wins, tying him with Bobby Allison for third on the all-time win list. *International Motorsports Hall of Fame*

Dave Marcis took over the K&K Insurance Dodge when Bobby Isaac left the car. *International Motorsports Hall of Fame*

In 1976 David Pearson won 10 times in only 22 starts in his Wood Brothers Mercury. He primarily ran superspeedways, but he also won 2 road races that year, both at Riverside. *International Motorsports Hall of Fame*

engine it dramatically improves horsepower. The teams would typically conceal the canisters of nitrous oxide under the car's dashboard or inside the tubes that made up the roll cage. More and more people were getting caught using it and NASCAR again worried about the bad press. It seemed that cheating was all the media wanted to talk about. But the media's attention was diverted on the afternoon of February 15, 1976.

ABC was once again at Daytona to show the conclusion of the Daytona 500. During the race Richard Petty and David Pearson, the two winningest drivers in the sport's history, battled hard for the lead over the last 20 or so laps. In the final turn of the final lap, the two cars made contact, and both drivers lost it. Petty's car came to a rest ahead of Pearson, in the grass, 100 or so feet short of the finish line. Pearson's battered Mercury wound up at the entrance to pit road. But Pearson was able to get his car moving, and Petty could not. Pearson's car was going so slow when he crossed the finish that a Volkswagen Bug probably could have outrun it—but it was enough. This incredible finish captured the imagination of both the press and the fans and was one of the pivotal moments that launched the sport into the national spotlight.

Ford had only 1 win in 1976, but Mercury came through with 10 (again, all from David Pearson). However, it was Chevrolet that led the way with 13 wins. Dodge's performance was fading but it was still able to score 6 wins, with Dave Marcis and Richard Petty winning 3 races each.

1977

In 1977, it was all Cale Yarborough. Richard Petty, Benny Parsons, and Darrell Waltrip all had great seasons, but no one could hang with Yarborough.

Yarborough had nine wins in his 30 starts and an incredible 25 top-five finishes. He also finished every race he started, the first time that had happened since 1962. For his performance, Yarborough, driving a Junior Johnson

Chevrolet, won the Winston Cup Championship by scoring 5,000 points, a record to this day. Any of the runners-up might have won a championship had it been any other year. Richard Petty, in his last full year driving a Dodge, had five wins and 20 top-fives. Benny Parsons, in a Chevrolet, had four wins and also scored 20 top-fives.

Much of the action in 1977 centered on the battle between Darrell Waltrip and Cale Yarborough and on the two men's relationships with their car owners. Waltrip and Yarborough were not the best of friends, and the intense competition on the track did not help matters. They had raced hard against each other all year, but the situation began to rear its head at Darlington during the Southern 500.

Waltrip and Yarborough had the best cars and battled all day. Between them they led the race 20 times, primarily swapping the lead between each other. Toward the end of the race, they went into the turn together and neither driver backed off. The result was a five-car pile-up.

The stock cars of the 1960s were basically production cars that were modified for racing. In the 1970s the race cars became more of a hybrid of stock and custom-built racer. *International Motorsports Hall of Fame*

race had 100 more laps. In reference to Yarborough's complaint, he claimed the problem was that Yarborough was just getting old.

Meanwhile, the two drivers were experiencing in-house problems as well. Yarborough led the points for the first 17 races, but when he lost the points lead to Richard Petty in midseason, he began to complain that his Junior Johnson–prepared Chevrolet was not quite up to par.

In fact, he claimed that he was driving the sorriest Chevrolet at the track. Johnson countered by basically telling Yarborough to shut up, or he might not have to worry about driving one of his cars. Likewise, things were not completely pleasant at the DiGard shop. Waltrip was not pleased by many of the staffing and in-house decisions and, like Yarborough, he was not shy about voicing his opinion.

Bobby Allison was making another change in 1977. Allison had started the 1974 season in a Chevrolet, winning in it at Richmond, the third race of the season. Later in the year he switched to a Roger Penske–prepared AMC Matador and won again late in the season, a 500-miler in Ontario. He won three more times in 1975 but was shut out in the 1976 season.

Before the 1977 season, Allison made the surprising announcement that he would be leaving Penske and preparing his own Matadors. He was again winless in 1977, scoring only 5 top-5 finishes and 15 top-10 finshes. That was enough for Allison, who in 1978 signed on to drive Bud Moore's Ford. It got Allison back in the winner's circle. He won five times and had 22 top-10 finishes in the 1978 season, and finished second in the points.

Another point of interest in the 1977 season was when the women showed up in force at Daytona. Janet Guthrie, Lella Lombardi, and Christine Beckers all drove in the Firecracker 400 on July 4.

David Pearson and Mercury were held to only two wins in 1977. Dodge stayed about the same as the year before with seven wins. Five of these came from Richard Petty and two more came from newcomer Neil Bonnett. In 1977 it was Chevrolet's turn to come on strong under the guidance of four drivers. Cale Yarborough had nine wins, Benny Parsons had four, Darrell Waltrip had six, and Donnie Allison added two more.

1978

As the 1978 season started, some of the cars running around the track were getting quite old. NASCAR rules allowed teams to run cars up to three years old. For instance,

Allison dropped the AMC Matador and went to work driving for Bud Moore. The Ford Thunderbird was still a boxy affair, and its only success of the 1978 season came with Allison at the wheel. Bobby won five times for Bud Moore, but was usually outpaced by the Chevrolets. *International Motorsports Hall of Fame*

After the race neither driver was happy, although both managed top-10 runs. It was after this race that Yarborough gave Waltrip the nickname "Jaws" because of Waltrip's ability to orate. Things were getting personal.

A few races later Waltrip would get his shot in. Yarborough won the race at Martinsville and in victory proclaimed that the 500-lap distance should be cut as he was completely exhausted after the race and he felt that it was dangerous to drive under those conditions.

The next week Waltrip won the 500-lap race at North Wilkesboro, another half-mile track. After the race he brashly commented that he felt great and wished that the

Richard Petty successfully ran his 1974 Dodge Charger in 1974, 1975, and 1976.

NASCAR had extended the eligibility of the 1974 models another 12 months, allowing them to be run again in 1977. The reason behind this was the inevitable downsizing of the cars. Since the fuel crisis had begun, the price of gas had doubled. The automakers in Detroit were beginning to lose sales to small imports from Toyota, Datsun (now Nissan), and Volkswagen. The big lumbering brutes produced by Detroit offered little in the way of fuel economy, and their future was bleak.

NASCAR allowed the teams to run the 74 models in 1977 because they knew that the race cars would be downsized when the production cars were. Delaying the change would shield the teams from the expense of preparing another "big" car when they would soon be changing to a downsized car anyway.

Before the 1978 season began, NASCAR again extended the older big cars' eligibility by 12 months. It would happen again and again, with the downsized cars not making their appearance until 1981.

Another landmark rule change allowed the Chevrolet motor, the GM-LM1 350, to be run in Buicks, Oldsmobiles, and Pontiacs. Many teams had switched to the Oldsmobile 442 because they felt it would be the best car aerodynamically. Now that it could carry the potent Chevrolet engine, it would be a formidable match.

For the Dodge teams, the new ride was the Magnum. The only fast thing about the car was the name, and the Mopar teams were not happy. They had wanted the Dodge Diplomat to be approved, but it was too small. NASCAR had announced that downsizing would be delayed and that the series would still be running big cars in 1978. The Magnum was so bad that in August 1978, Richard Petty showed up for the Michigan race with a Chevrolet Monte Carlo.

There was also a rule change concerning spoilers. The rule had been that the height of the spoiler had to be 3 inches. The problem with this was that cars with a wider deck lid had a spoiler with more surface area. The new rule

would balance the entire field by mandating that the spoiler could be a maximum of 190 square inches.

An interesting side story in the 1978 season is that of Willy T. Ribbs. Ribbs was a California road racer and, with the help of Humpy Wheeler, he was to drive a Will Cronkrite–owned race car in a Winston Cup race. Two days of private practice were scheduled at Charlotte for Ribbs to become acclimated to the car, which was far heavier than he was accustomed to running.

Ribbs did not show up for either practice session, but he did manage to be ticketed for going the wrong way down a one-way street in Charlotte while he was missing practice. Since he did not practice, his entry in the race was denied. Cronkrite suddenly needed a driver for the Charlotte race. He settled on an unproven local sportsman driver by the name of Dale Earnhardt. Earnhardt ran well and finished the race, securing himself a ride for the next season.

Cale Yarborough switched from Chevrolet to Oldsmobile and had 10 wins. Lennie Pond added another win to bring Oldsmobile's total to 11. Benny Parsons, Darrell Waltrip, and Donnie Allison stayed with Chevrolet and racked up 10 total wins. Bobby Allison won 5 times in a Ford, which would be the only Ford wins in 1978. And good

The last effort for Dodge was the Magnum. It proved to be a dismal race car, due to its design and lack of power. The strong commitment to racing that had supported the Mopar effort for so many years had disappeared. Here Kyle Petty tries to get as much as he can out of the Magnum. The Magnum was so bad that it resulted in Richard Petty moving to General Motors' products. The Senior Petty had driven his last NASCAR race in a Mopar product. *International Motorsports Hall of Fame*

old David Pearson kept the Mercury camp winning with 4 wins in 1978. Dodge was shut out. In fact, the last win of the twentieth century for Dodge came at Ontario in the last race of the 1977 season.

1979

The sport achieved another milestone in 1979 when, for the first time, fans could sit in the comfort of their homes and watch the entire Daytona 500. CBS had decided to expand its coverage and show the entire race. This was a good choice for CBS and a great break for NASCAR. As the laps wound down, Cale Yarborough and

Donnie Allison battled at the front. Allison was driving a Hoss Ellington Oldsmobile and Yarborough was driving for Junior Johnson, who had also switched to an Oldsmobile. On the final lap, Yarborough and Allison got together on the back straightaway and both crashed. Richard Petty drove through the carnage and won the race, his first victory in 45 starts.

After finishing 11th in his Ford, Bobby Allison stopped at the site of the accident to check on his brother. Bobby Allison and Yarborough swapped words, and then Yarborough took a swing at Bobby Allison. Yarborough was angry because he felt that Bobby Allison, who was three laps down, had blocked for his brother. After the race NASCAR agreed and placed Bobby Allison on probation.

While it was not the sport's finest moment, the sensational nature of the finish captivated both fans and the media. Television ratings for the race were high. In fact, the 1979 Daytona 500 was the top-rated show for each and every half-hour of its broadcast, according to the Nielsen rating system. During the race the ratings increased each hour with an incredibly high 13.5 rating for the final half-hour. The entire broadcast had a 10.5 rating, and CBS won an Emmy for the broadcast.

Another milestone of the 1979 season was when David Pearson drove his last race for the Wood Brothers in the spring race at Darlington. Things had become strained between the driver and team, and a pit miscue was the last straw. During a pit stop, Pearson thought that he was only getting two tires but the pit crew was putting

on four. Leonard Wood called out "Whoa" on the radio but Pearson thought that he said, "Go," and sped away. Unfortunately, he had no lug nuts on the left side wheels, and both fell off.

But Pearson would win one more race. He won the Southern 500, the second race of the year at Darlington, in Ron Osterlund's Chevrolet. Pearson was the substitute driver for the injured Dale Earnhardt. It was Pearson's 104th win in NASCAR's highest division.

When the dust settled on the 1979 season, Richard Petty had won his seventh and last championship. Petty made up a 187-point deficit in seven races to edge Darrell Waltrip by only 11 points.

As one great driver won his last award, a newcomer was winning his first. Despite sitting out four races with injuries, Dale Earnhardt won Rookie-of-the-Year honors, beating Harry Gant and Terry Labonte. Earnhardt finished seventh in the Winston Cup Championship with one win in 27 starts. His one victory, his first career win, came at Bristol on April 1 in his Ron Osterlund Chevrolet.

In 1979, Chevrolet's winning ways continued. Darrell Waltrip was the biggest Chevrolet winner with 7 victories in his DiGard ride. At season's end, Chevrolet had 18 wins and Oldsmobile had 5. Neil Bonnett took over the driving duties in the Wood Brothers Mercury and scored 3 wins for the brand. Bobby Allison was again the only man to win in a Ford, piloting Bud Moore's Ford to 5 wins. The 1979 cars were just carryovers from 1978. Everyone knew that a big, costly change to downsized cars was coming, however.

Three of the great ones are lined up for service. David Pearson, Richard Petty, and Dale Earnhardt would end up with 380 combined career wins. For most of their wins, Pearson drove a Mercury, Petty a Dodge or Plymouth, and Earnhardt a Chevrolet. *International Motorsports Hall of Fame*

As the 1980s began, Dodge, Plymouth, and Chrysler were gone. The show was now between General Motors and Ford. Mercury would win once in 1980 and would never visit victory lane again. *International Motorsports Hall of Fame*

The 1980s

As the 1980s began, the sport was on a roll. It was still gaining in popularity, and as television coverage expanded, more fans were coming aboard. The sport would change more in the 1980s than any time in its history. Cars would lose most of their "stock" ties in the 1980s. The biggest connection to the factory would be the body's sheet metal, but by the late 1980s this too would change. They were becoming true race cars. The fuel that fed the fire was increased television coverage. Cable television meant that, by the end of the decade, a fan could watch almost every race, in its entirety, from the comfort of his or her living room.

This accessibility would boost the sport, making it one of the most popular in the country by the late 1980s and early 1990s.

After winning Rookie-of-the-Year honors in 1979, Dale Earnhardt didn't wait for long to become a major factor in the sport. On March 16 at Atlanta, he won his first superspeedway race. In doing so, he outran another newcomer to the sport, Rusty Wallace, who was competing in his first Winston Cup race.

Wallace was impressive right off the bat, finishing a close second. Earnhardt ran well all year and won the championship after a close struggle with Cale Yarborough. Earnhardt won a total of five races and had 19 top-five finishes, while Yarborough won six races and also had 19 top-fives. While it was a close battle all year, Earnhardt topped the points table from the second race until the end of the year.

Richard Petty was a bit off of the pace in 1980, finishing fourth in the points. Part of the reason was that Petty suffered a broken neck in a crash at Pocono (while leading) during the 19th race of the season. Petty would start the next race, but would require a relief driver. By the following race, however, the tough North Carolina driver resumed full-time driving duties.

Some big-name drivers were jumping rides at the end of the 1980 season. One of the big changes occurred when Cale Yarborough left his formidable Junior Johnson Chevrolet. Yarborough had decided that he wanted to run a limited schedule, but in an MC Anderson Buick. Johnson had to find a driver and chose the brash Darrell Waltrip. When Waltrip left the DiGard No. 88 Chevrolet, the team landed another great driver in Ricky Rudd. DiGard also switched to a Buick for the 1981 season.

General Motors started the new decade well with 22 wins from Chevrolet and 3 wins from Oldsmobile. The hot Chevrolet ride was the Monte Carlo, with a 358-cubic-inch engine. The suspension featured fabricated control arms, coil springs, twin shocks and a sway bar in the front, and coil springs, a Panhard bar, trailing arms, and a Ford 9-inch rear end at the back.

Power was beginning to creep up in the small blocks. The early versions had only been able to put out around 500 horsepower. By the early 1980s they were over 600 and climbing. While Chevrolet was having success after success, the Ford Motor Company was bottoming out. In 1980 it dropped to 4 wins from Ford and 2 from Mercury.

1981

After years of waiting, the small cars finally arrived in 1981. They had been talked about since the mid-1970s, but it had taken until 1981 to make the change. As of the Daytona race, the 110-inch-wheelbase cars would be used instead of the old-wheelbase cars, which ranged from 115 to 118 inches. After the fuel crisis of the 1970s, Detroit had downsized its cars and NASCAR was now following suit.

For the teams and drivers, a shorter wheelbase meant a shorter body, which in turn meant different aerodynamic properties. A shorter wheelbase would also change the handling characteristics of the car; the suspension setup that worked on a longer-wheelbase car wasn't necessarily so good under the shorter car. The problem was that the cars had just as much horsepower and speed as before, but the teams were all starting from scratch in the setup department.

The small-wheelbase models approved for racing were the Buick Regal, Chevrolet Monte Carlo, Chevrolet Malibu, Chrysler LeBaron, Dodge Mirada, Ford Thunderbird, Ford Granada, Mercury Cougar XR-7, Mercury Monarch, Oldsmobile Cutlass Supreme, Pontiac Grand Prix, and Pontiac LeMans. The teams had a lot of cars to choose from, but the problems were stout.

The big change in the 1980s took place when the "small" cars replaced the "big" cars. The wheelbase was cut from 115–118 inches to a strict 110 inches. Here, Benny Parsons practices in the new Bud Moore Ford. Everything changed when the wheelbase and body were shortened, so the crew chiefs almost had to start from scratch learning new setups. *International Motorsports Hall of Fame*
Below: The 1981 Pontiac Le Mans brought about a rule change that exists to this day. All cars had previously run the same size spoiler, but the aerodynamic advantage (due to the slope of the rear glass) of the Le Mans led to different makes having different spoiler sizes. *Don Hunter*

After one practice session in the new cars, Bobby Allison announced that in terms of handling, they had only been able to take a horrible car and make it simply bad. Petty again tried the Dodge product, but after testing his Mirada was well off of the pace of the General Motors cars.

The new cars were accompanied by a new spoiler rule. NASCAR moved away from a standard size of spoiler and allowed different spoilers for different brands of cars. The rule was primarily aimed to slow down the Pontiac LeMans. Bobby Allison was the only driver in a LeMans, but the slope of its rear window made the car arguably the best out there.

NASCAR, as always, sought to level the playing field. Allison's viewpoint was that they were competing within the rules, and that they had worked hard and taken chances with a car no one else wanted. Just as soon as they could realize the benefits of their work and decisions, they had the rug pulled out from under them. But NASCAR wanted balance, and balance it would get.

The new cars seemed to take their toll on Dale Earnhardt. After winning five times in 1980, Earnhardt went winless in 1981. His team owner, Rod Osterlund, sold the team midway through the season to J. D. Stacey. In August, Earnhardt quit the team and accepted the job of driving the rest of the year for Richard Childress. Childress had been a driver for 12 years, but he changed overnight from driver to car owner. For the remaining 11 races of the 1981 season, Earnhardt and Childress worked on the new team. The pairing showed promise, as the two managed two top-five finishes before the season was over. As this legendary partnership began, another legendary partnership was coming to an end. Long-time crew chief Dale Inman left Richard Petty.

General Motors once again dominated the year, but Chevrolet was no longer its top make. The previous year, Chevy had won 22 races, but the new bodies did not favor them and in 1981 they only to managed 1 win. However, Buick came on strong with 22 wins. Pontiac also had a single win in 1981. Ford's winning percentage was up a bit as it won 7 times.

Another big moment for the promotion of NASCAR came in 1981. The cable television business was growing and a new network, the Entertainment Sports Programming Network (ESPN), televised the Atlanta Journal 500 live. It also announced its intention to televise more events in 1982. ESPN and later TNN (The Nashville Network) would play a huge role in the terrific growth of the sport during the 1980s and 1990s. While such major networks as CBS and ABC might have been carrying the big events at the big tracks, NASCAR's short-track events were not likely to be seen on television. These cable networks, by covering a larger portion of the schedule, would ultimately allow fans all over the country to see the full diversity of tracks and driving that NASCAR had to offer.

1982

In 1982 Darrell Waltrip joined an elite group of drivers by winning back-to-back championships, but it was not easy. Waltrip had to make up a 147-point deficit to Bobby

Allison in the last seven events. Allison was now driving for the DiGard team in a Buick and had started the year off with a win at Daytona.

Allison's bumper was knocked off of the car on the fourth lap of the race, but it seemed to have no effect; in fact, some said that it increased the car's performance. Allison was accused of intentionally fixing the car so that the bumper would drop off, but it could not be proven and nothing ever came of the accusations. Allison got the DiGard ride after Ricky Rudd left to drive for Richard Childress. The Childress ride, now a Pontiac, was open after Dale Earnhardt left to drive one of Bud Moore's Fords.

During the year, Buick continued to dominate, and Ford continued to struggle. Buick won an impressive 25 times and Chevrolet added 3 more wins to give General Motors a winning percentage of 93.3 (28 wins out of 30 races). Ford was only able to squeak out 2 wins, at Darlington with Dale Earnhardt in Bud Moore's Ford, and at Charlotte with Neil Bonnett in the Wood Brothers Ford. Darrell Waltrip won

The Buick was General Motors' biggest winner in 1981. Buicks won 22 of the season's 31 races. Here newcomer Tim Richmond pilots his Buick through a turn. Richmond ran 29 races in 1981 and had six top-10 finishes. *Don Hunter*

All of the teams were becoming more comfortable with the smaller cars, but Ford still needed to do something to regain its position in the sport. It would begin the climb back in 1983 with the introduction of the new, more aerodynamic Thunderbird. It would not be a blockbuster success right off the bat, but over time it would prove to be one of the greatest NASCAR rides ever.

1983

As the 1983 season got under way, cheating once again became an issue. This time the biggest scandal centered on Richard Petty and Petty Enterprises.

Petty hadn't won a race since early in the previous

the championship winning 12 races, and Bobby Allison finished second with 8 wins. Terry Labonte also had a fine year in the Billy Hagen Buick, finishing third in the points. Although he had no wins, he did have 17 top-five finishes in 30 starts.

year, and he spent a good bit of this time telling his brother and engine builder, Maurice, that he needed more horsepower. At Charlotte for the Miller High Life 500, Maurice gave him more power in the form of a very illegal 381-cubic-inch engine (23 cubic inches bigger than the

The DiGard team's new 1982 Monte Carlo. The DiGard team had many great drivers, including Darrell Waltrip. *International Motorsports Hall of Fame*

358-cubic-inch limit). The engine passed the prerace inspection with its valves wedged open with wax, which fooled the air test that the NASCAR inspectors used. Once the race started, the wax melted away and off Petty went. Petty started 20th and made a late charge to win the event.

That wasn't all Petty pulled. During the last pit stop, the crew fitted left-side tires, which were softer than the right-side tires, on both sides of the car. This too was illegal. Tim Richmond had been penalized five laps in an earlier race for the same infraction, and in all likelihood it had cost him a win.

Everyone associated with the postrace inspection was trying to figure out how to handle the tire infraction when Maurice confessed that the engine was illegal as well.

When NASCAR measured it, the engine displaced 381.983 cubic inches.

In this case, the masses would not have to wait long for a ruling. After only three hours, Petty was fined a then-record $35,000 and stripped of 104 points. He was, however, allowed to keep the win. NASCAR had always tried to let the winner be decided on the track.

This incident became a hotbed of discussion in stock car racing circles. How bad was the cheating throughout the field? If the King was cheating, what else was going on? Nowhere was the situation discussed more than among NASCAR officials.

Shortly after the Charlotte incident, NASCAR announced a new rule. Anyone caught running an oversized

motor would be subject to a suspension of 12 weeks or three races.

At the end of the year, Richard left Petty Enterprises to drive the Curb Motorsports Pontiac. He stated that his reason for leaving was the burden of running his and son Kyle's cars out of the same shop. However, many wondered what effect the Charlotte episode had on the decision.

Other notes of interest during the 1983 season included Cale Yarborough becoming the first driver to break the 200-mile-per-hour mark in qualifying at Daytona. His first lap speed was 200.503 miles per hour, but he crashed on his second lap. Mark Martin, a newcomer to the circuit, had been fired by the J. D. Stacy team and replaced by Morgan Shepherd. Martin fielded his own effort in 1982 with help from Bud Reeder. He would bounce around the remainder of the 1983 season, driving the Ulrich Racing Buick, the Emanuel Zervakis Chevrolet, and the Morgan McClure Oldsmobile in selected races.

Another relatively new driver was also making a name for himself. Bill Elliot ran every race on the circuit for the first time and was rewarded with a third-place finish in the championship. In the points race, Bobby Allison finally outlasted Darrell Waltrip and won the championship.

Allison and Waltrip both finished the year with six wins in 30 starts.

While General Motors would again dominate the 1983 season, the favorite ride again was the Chevrolet. Buick still had 6 wins and Pontiac came through with 5, but Chevys won 15 times. Ford showed progress by doubling its wins from the previous year with 4 total wins. While the Fords were not dominating by any stretch of the imagination, the General Motors guys were nonetheless keeping an eye on them. Even without strong factory backing, the new Thunderbirds were impressive.

The Chevrolet Monte Carlo being fielded by the GM guys had many good points, but it had a few bad points as well. Most of the bad points centered once again on the car's aerodynamic efficiency. The nose of the Monte Carlo had been lengthened and dropped somewhat to help this problem.

When Cale Yarborough ripped off a NASCAR's first official 200-mile-per-hour lap and shortly thereafter went tumbling down the track (he was OK), the core problems of the Monte Carlo body were put in plain view. While the front of the car was very aerodynamic, the conventional, near-vertical rear window created problems.

continued on page 119

In the early 1980s Ford teams were struggling because of weak factory support, but relief was in sight. While only moderately successful, the new Thunderbird's sleek body represented the shape of things to come. One of the biggest differences was the return to a sloped rear window.
Here Buddy Baker pilots the Wood Brothers Thunderbird. *Don Hunter*

The Chassis

The first racers relied on the factories for their chassis. The cars of the 1950s were full-framed, meaning the body was bolted to a strong steel frame, much like a modern pickup truck. This meant that the bottom of the car was pretty strong, but the sides and top were a bit weak. *International Motorsports Hall of Fame*

The modern Winston Cup chassis provides protection that early drivers could only dream of. The steel skeleton of the chassis makes up the backbone of the car. The accuracy and repeatability inherent in the construction of the chassis are critical. Accuracy is of obvious importance. The finished product must be within the specifications of the team and the specifications of NASCAR. Every piece must go together correctly. The pieces must be the right size, and all of the welded connections must be in the right places. By clamping the chassis pieces into a fixture during assembly, any problem can be identified, and mistakes will be caught before they are made permanent.

Repeatability is also important, because the team must have control over every chassis if its track notes are to mean anything. Crew chiefs keep extensive notes of all setups that have been run at each track. Every adjustment made to the car during practice sessions and races, and the result of each particular adjustment, is noted. They also record track conditions, such as temperature, humidity, cloud cover, wind direction, and speed.

Roll bars were the first step in the move toward a race-specific chassis. For the first few years of NASCAR racing, roll bars were not mandatory. Even if they were present, they were often not much help. Some early roll-bar materials included 2x4s and old plumbing pipe. *International Motorsports Hall of Fame*

building of the chassis. Occasionally, bars must pass through the sheet metal floor pan to the frame rails. Where this happens, holes are cut in the sheet metal to allow the bars to pass through. All other sheet-metal pieces are added after the chassis is completed.

The front subframe is the structure that extends from the firewall to the front of the car. The rules require that it must extend from the lower radiator support (in the front) to the forward edge of the front frame rails (in the rear). The mounting positions for the steering and the engine are located on the front subframe. The width of the main subframe rails must be a minimum of 29 inches at the steering box and must be parallel to the centerline of the car. The inside width measured at the engine block may not exceed 34 inches. Suspension fittings are also built into the front subassembly.

In the 1960s the cars began to sport a more complete cage for driver protection. At the beginning of the decade, the bars were welded into the car. Later in the decade, the teams began to disassemble the car, build the roll cage, and weld the car to the bars. International Motorsports Hall of Fame

By the 1970s and 1980s the cars were much safer for the driver in case of an accident. The roll cage was becoming a stronger and stronger unit. More bars meant more strength. International Motorsports Hall of Fame

For these notes to mean anything, each chassis must be identical, or the crew chief must be aware of any differences built into the chassis so that he may take them into account when setting up the race car.

The chassis is made up of four main parts: the frame rails, the roll cage, the front subframe, and the rear subframe. The foundation of the chassis is the frame rails, which are made from rectangular steel tubing. Once the frame rails have been fabricated, the assembly of the roll cage begins. The roll cage is the primary contributor to driver safety. Many feet of steel tubing are blended to achieve one goal: strength. Avoiding injuries—during the tremendous impacts that are possible when racing—is dependent on the brute strength of the steel roll cage.

There are many structural bars in a Winston Cup roll cage including horizontal bars, vertical bars, and a couple of support bars that run diagonally. All of these bars are made from round, magnetic seamless steel tubing with a 1-3/4-inch diameter and a .090-inch wall thickness (meeting ASTM A-519 specifications).

The firewall, the floor pan, and the rear wheelwells are the primary sheet-metal pieces added during the

The modern stock car is built around a steel roll cage/chassis that is completely assmebled before the teams mount the body. The chassis is made of rectangular frame rails, the roll cage, the front clip, and the rear clip. Damage to the front or rear clip can often be repaired if the car is in a crash.

The modern chassis allows most drivers to escape tremendous accidents without life-threatening injuries. Bill Elliot got pretty banged up in this 200-mile-per-hour Talladega crash but was back racing before the season was over.

For the finished car to handle properly, all of these fittings must be positioned correctly. A mistake at this point could mean a handling problem to overcome on the track. The rear subframe extends rearward from the back of the main frame rails, up and over the rear axle, and back down to hold the fuel cell. It includes the mounting points for the rear springs, shocks, Panhard bar (track bar), sway bar, and fuel cell.

At any point along the rear subframe rails, the distance from the centerline must be the same on each side. The rear subframe must maintain a minimum width of 37 inches at the fuel cell mounting location.

When the bare chassis is complete, it is delivered to the body fabrication shop, where the body will be made and mounted.

Continued from page 115

As the air flowed over the back edge of the roof, it became very turbulent. The air could not flow smoothly to the deck lid, and the result was lift. At high speed, this lifting effect was so great that it could actually lift the rear tires from the track. This is precisely what happened to Yarborough. The Monte Carlo would soon change again.

1984

As the 1984 season kicked into gear at Daytona, a number of drivers had changed rides once again. Ricky Rudd and Dale Earnhardt would swap rides as Earnhardt returned to the Childress team and Rudd moved to the Bud Moore Ford. Darrell Waltrip was still with Johnson, but now he had a teammate in the person of Neil Bonnett.

Richard Petty, driving the Curb Motorsports Pontiac, got his 199th win on May 20 at Dover Downs. He was only one win away from 200 when the teams returned to Daytona for the second time in the 1984 season. Petty had broken a cam early in the Daytona 500 at the beginning of the year and was hoping for better results in this second trip to the track.

The race turned into a duel between Petty and Cale Yarborough, but Petty outlasted him and got his 200th win. One of the fans in attendance was President Ronald Reagan. The President and the King had a moment to share their thoughts with each other after the race.

The points race was tight in 1984. The biggest lead anyone had all year was 91 points. When the smoke cleared after the 30th and last race of the year, Terry Labonte had won his first championship by 65 points over Harry Gant.

Labonte, driving a Billy Hagan Chevrolet, had won two races during the year, while Gant captured three. Bill Elliot was again third with three wins, Dale Earnhardt was fourth with two wins, and Darrell Waltrip was fifth with seven.

The General Motors pendulum continued to swing away from Buick and back toward Chevrolet. Buick was held to 2 wins while Chevrolets took 21 checkered flags. Pontiac also won 3 times, bringing the General Motors total to 26. Ford once again struggled and had only 4 wins.

1985

Winning became a lot more lucrative in 1985. Series sponsor R. J. Reynolds upped the prize money significantly for both individual race purses and championship rewards. Two other special programs were added. The first was a new "all star" event that would be run at Charlotte for all drivers who had won the previous year. It would be called "The Winston" and would prove to be an action-packed, no-holds-barred event that the fans would grow to love. The second special program offered a $1 million bonus to any driver who could win three of the four biggest races on the circuit: the Daytona 500, the Winston 500 at Talladega, the Southern 500 at Darlington, and the World 600 at Charlotte. The races represented the richest, the fastest, the oldest, and the longest events on the NASCAR schedule.

Bill Elliot dominated in 1985, but it wasn't enough to win the championship.

Elliot's run began at Daytona practice, where no one else could equal the times that Elliot's Ford Thunderbird was posting. While a few drivers were barely breaking the 200-miles-per-hour barrier, Elliot was posting times over 202 miles per hour. Some (mainly the Chevy guys) complained that the Fords had an unfair aerodynamic advantage because they were allowed to run an inch lower than the Chevrolets.

When qualifying rolled around, Elliot clocked a lap at 205.114 miles per hour to take the pole. Elliot led 136 of the

In the 1970s and 1980s, Junior Johnson built one of the best rides on the Winston Cup circuit. In the mid-1980s he had both Darrell Waltrip and Neil Bonnett driving his Monte Carlos.
International Motorsports Hall of Fame

By the mid-1980s, Bobby Allison and DiGard had moved to Buicks. Bobby Allison drove this 1984 Buick to two wins in the 1984 season. *International Motorsports Hall of Fame*

race's 200 laps, while many top cars blew motors trying to keep up with him. He won the race and was a third of the way to the million-dollar bonus.

Elliot and the other Fords lost a bit of their advantage when, effective April 29, the roof height for all cars was changed to 50.5 inches. The Fords would have to be raised a half-inch and the GM cars lowered a half-inch.

The first race to be run after the rules change was the Winston 500 at Talladega. Elliot still had something special, qualifying at 209.398 miles per hour, while Cale Yarborough was second-fastest at "only" 205.679 miles per hour.

During the race, Elliot and his Thunderbird put on a show. On lap 48 Elliot's car began to stream a thick cloud of

smoke. Elliot pitted under the green flag and the crew fixed a broken oil fitting. The long pit stop put Elliot almost three laps (about 5 miles) behind the leaders. With no cautions to help, Elliot drove his Ford like a madman, and on lap 145 he retook the lead and went on to win the race. He was two-for-two in the big events and a win in the Southern 500 or the World 600 would be worth an additional million dollars.

The next big one was at Charlotte. Elliot won the pole for the World 600, but brake failure relegated him to an 18th-place finish. Darrell Waltrip won the race and also won the inaugural Winston the day before the 600.

Elliot's last chance at the million would be at Darlington in the Southern 500. He again won the pole, but

In 1985, Elliot became the first to win Winston's $1 million bonus, as he drove his Thunderbird to victory in three out of the season's four biggest races: the Daytona 500, the Winston 500 at Talladega, the Southern 500 at Darlington, and the World 600 at Charlotte. The four are the richest, the fastest, the oldest, and the longest NASCAR events. *International Motorsports Hall of Fame*

as the day went by he was not racing well. He caught a break when, as he was about to go a lap down, a caution flag came out. The crew adjusted the chassis and things got much better. He fought his way back to the front and, in the final stages of the race, Elliot battled Cale Yarborough for the win. Elliot won at the wire by a little over half a second and the million was his.

Aside from his three wins in the four biggest races of the year, Elliot won eight other superspeedway events. Darrell Waltrip won only three times in 1985, but was more consistent over the course of the season. When the year ended Elliot, finished second to Waltrip by 101 points in the championship race.

Ford had a rebirth in 1985, thanks to the better-refined Thunderbird and Bill Elliot, but between rival manufacturers it was a dead heat. Both Chevrolet and Ford won 14 times. Buick, which had been so strong over the past few years, along with Pontiac and Oldsmobile, was shut out.

The cars were becoming more and more sophisticated. Many more aftermarket parts were appearing from the manufacturers, and many of the stock bits would soon disappear. In 1985 Gary Nelson, a top crew chief with 21 race wins in 258 starts, prepared a car with parts that NASCAR was considering making legal, including engine and suspension parts that NASCAR itself was testing. The car was so good that Greg Sacks drove it to win the Firecracker 400 at Daytona.

1986

The fix for the Monte Carlo's aerodynamic problem was unveiled in 1986 with the Monte Carlo SS Aero Coupe. The major change was a "bubble"-style rear glass that provided a much smoother transition for the air spilling off the roof of the car. Chevrolet made enough of the cars to be considered a production car, so it could be raced. The results were impressive. In the 1986 and 1987 seasons these cars won 33 of 58 races under the control of many different drivers.

The car was also changing beneath the skin. A new development in the car's suspension was the single shock per wheel. With gas shocks, only one was necessary. This made the team's lives easier, as is harder to balance the force of two shocks when setting up a car than a single shock.

continued on page 125

Tires

The tire is literally where the rubber meets the road—it's the biggest factor in deciding how a modern stock car handles. So it is also, perhaps, the most important linkage in the suspension of a stock car. As a 3,400-pound car flies through a turn at 170 miles per hour, the amount of tire touching the ground at any one time is relatively small (about four times the size of my size 11-1/2 hiking boot). It is this small patch of contact that keeps the Goodyear engineers and the crew chiefs very busy.

The first thing a tire has to do is not go to pieces. This has been a problem over the history of the sport, and it occasionally still surfaces. The car's tires are under a tremendous amount of stress. As the car goes through a turn, forces try to throw it to the outside of the turn. The tire is the component that stops this from happening.

The tires' soft rubber and heavy sidewall construction allow the cars to achieve such high speeds in the turns. Friction between the racing surface and the tire heats the rubber. The right amount of heat enables the tires to "glue" the car to the track, up to a point. Too little heat, and the tire won't grip the way the driver expects. Too much heat can do the same, and can even destroy the tire.

As the tire wears and builds up more and more heat, it gradually begins to lose its gripping ability, and lap times begin to drop. Tire wear differs depending on the type of track being raced. Tracks like Darlington eat tires up, while the surface at Talladega doesn't.

Early cars ran ordinary street tires, but as the sport progressed, the strain of racing became too much for them. Companies began to offer special racing tires for competitors.

In the NASCAR ranks, the Pure Oil Company was the first to offer a race-only tire. They were much narrower than the modern race tire and still had treads. Firestone came into the sport in the 1950s and competed with some success until the late 1960s. After Firestone's withdrawal, the cars were shod with Goodyears. Hoosier began competing in the late 1980s and also enjoyed some success. At the time of its entrance into the sport, Hoosier had 18 full-time employees, against Goodyear's 350,000. Hoosier's tenure was short, though, as it left the sport in 1989, just as Goodyear was introducing the racing radial.

Before the radial, racing tires had been made with a bias-ply construction technique. Bias-ply tires were not nearly as stable as the radial tire—they would change during a run. As the tire wore and the heat increased, the diameter of the tire tended to increase. This made the ideal car setup a moving target for the teams. A tire that might work reliably during a five-lap stint would change during a 50-lap run. As each tire was experiencing different conditions (the right front takes much more abuse than the left rear), they would grow at different rates, so the stagger (the difference in tire size from one side of the car to the other) and air pressure would constantly change.

Drivers who ran the bias-ply tires had to deal with this on just about every lap of every race. The car might handle well for 10 laps, bad for 15, and then behave well again. The result was that during much of the actual racing on bias-ply tires, the car would not enjoy its ideal setup, and the driver would have to rely on his skill to "manhandle" the car around the race track. Hence, when running bias-ply tires, driver skill was at a premium.

Everything changed with the radial. In a bias-ply tire the cords, which give the tire its strength, were run at an angle from bead to bead. On a radial tire the cords run straight across the tread from bead to bead. This difference in construction has a huge impact on how the tire behaves when it is being raced. The radial does not grow and as a result puts much more of the burden on the suspension and geometry of the car.

When the sport began to use radials, the teams encountered a new situation. For years, the control of the setup and the geometry of the car were not as important, as the setup would be changing during the course of a run anyway. Radials did build-up heat, which changed the air pressure and stiffened the tire up, just like putting more spring in the car. But other than that, the tires remained stable.

By the 1970s Goodyear was the primary supplier of racing tires, and the tires' tread was now grooveless. The tires were known as bias-plies and they served the racers well for years. Bias-ply construction means that the belts in the tire are laid from side to side at 45-degree angles. But as the tires got hotter during a run, they grew in diameter. As each tire was experiencing different stresses and different amounts of heat, the four tires on the car would grow at different rates. *International Motorsports Hall of Fame*

The racing radial came to Winston Cup racing as the 1990s started. It took Goodyear a while to develop the radial tire for racing and work out all the problems, but when it did, racers had a tire that would remain pretty much the same size throughout a run. In a radial construction, the belts in the tire run straight across the tires at a 90-degree angle from the bead.

Even with the new radials, the stress of racing can occasionally be too much for the tires. The crew chief must be aware of how much heat each tire is building up, reading the tire temperatures and adjusting the spring pressures to balance the heat. When doing this, they look at diagonal relationships, comparing the right front to the left rear and the left front to the right rear.

As a result, the setup would not change as much during long runs. Since the setup would remain pretty constant, it became more important to zero in on the best suspension setup. The car's design, assembly, and suspension tuning became more and more critical to the overall performance to the team. The teams began to work harder, in a more technical manner.

Now the cars that run well on long runs belong to the drivers who have the best setup. When the tires are new and sticky, a setup that is off a bit may run very well. This is often seen during a race. A car will be very fast for 20 or so laps and then begin to fade when the car cannot overcome its setup flaw. Races can be won with a setup like this, but the cautions must fall at the right times. The guys who have really nailed the setup will be the ones who run the more consistent laps throughout the run.

For those who say the old drivers were better than the current crop, this bias-ply versus radial difference is one of their principal arguments. I don't know. I think that with a time machine Jeff Gordon would win in the 1950s and Fireball Roberts would win in the 1990s. Bobby Allison and Dale Earnhardt would win in anything from chariots to space ships.

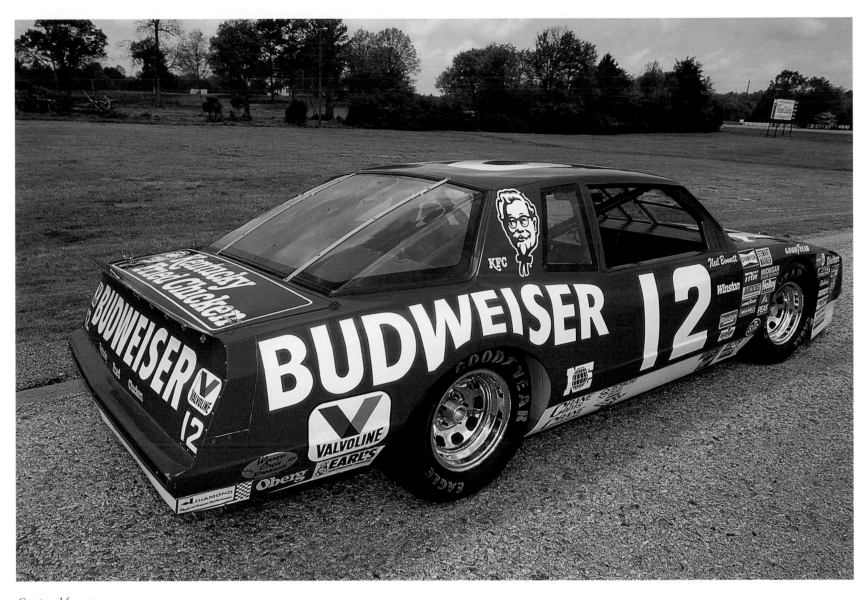

Continued from page 121

Perhaps in response to the aggressive stance that R. J. Reynolds took in sponsoring the sport, and following its increased activities during 1985, for the 1986 season NASCAR would drop the name Grand National for its premier series.

The series evolved from the Grand National Division, a name that Bill France Sr. had come up with in the early 1950s, to the Winston Cup Grand Nationals, and, finally, to the Winston Cup. The Grand National name was passed to the next series down the ladder, a series that would become the Busch Grand Nationals.

The races were as competitive as ever. One of the better examples took place at Richmond, when Darrell Waltrip and Dale Earnhardt were battling for the lead late in the race.

With three laps to go, Waltrip passed Earnhardt, and in the following turn Earnhardt made contact with Waltrip. Both cars spun, causing a huge crash that involved many of the top-running cars. Kyle Petty threaded his way through the wreckage, emerged as the leader, and took his first win. Earnhardt would be fined and put on probation for the incident, but in an appeal the penalties were lowered and the probation was dropped. Many saw this as this as a sellout by NASCAR, but the decision stood.

In the manufacturer's race the parity between Ford and General Motors did not last long. All four of the General Motors brands took checkered flags in 1986. Chevrolet won 18 times, Buick 3, Oldsmobile 1, and Pontiac 2, to give GM a total of 24 wins. Ford was only able to chalk up 5 wins.

For 1986 the Monte Carlo would add a "bubble style" rear window to the back of the car. This rather ugly piece of glass dramatically improved the airflow over the roof and down to the spoiler. The results were impressive as Chevrolet won 18 races in 1986, while Ford won only five times.

Dale Earnhardt won the championship with five wins, 16 top-5 finishes, and 23 top-10 finishes. Darrell Waltrip finished second with three wins, 21 top-5 finishes, and 22 top-10 finishes. However, the driver with the most wins in 1986 was Tim Richmond. Richmond had seven wins in 29 starts and finished third in the championship race. Richmond had come from racing open-wheel cars and had been named Rookie of the Year at the Indianapolis 500, but after a few bad crashes switched over to stock cars.

Tim was an incredibly talented driver and had already been in NASCAR for a few years. He ran in the 1980 and 1981 seasons without winning, but won twice in 1982 and 1983 and once again in 1984. He was again shut out in 1985, so he really turned heads with his success during 1986.

1987

Richmond drove eight races in 1987, winning at Pocono and Riverside. These would be his last wins. Tim retired from racing in 1987 because of health problems related to the AIDS virus. He died on August 7, 1989.

Another son of a popular driver joined the circuit in 1987. Davey Allison, Bobby's son, won Rookie-of-the-Year honors. He did so in an impressive way, winning two races in his Ranier–Lundy Ford.

At the end of the previous year, Ranier was losing driver Cale Yarborough and crew chief Waddell Wilson. Faced with the prospect of losing these two legends, he ended up hiring three men who were also destined to become legends. Davey Allison was named as the driver, Joey Knuckles would be crew chief, and Robert Yates was hired as the engine builder.

The team came together quickly, winning at Talladega on May 3, and at Dover on May 31. Allison ran in only 22 of the 29 races in 1987, but he still finished the year with 2 wins, 9 top-5 finishes, and 10 top-10 finishes.

While Davey was the hot newcomer, Dale Earnhardt was the hot veteran. Earnhardt dominated 1987. He had 11

Tim Richmond was brash and often unfocused, but no one could question his incredible skill behind the wheel. Tim won seven races in 1986. Tim left the sport when he got sick, but would come back for a Hollywood finish. Tim ran in eight events in 1987 and won two of them before leaving the sport for good. Tim's cars were prepared by the legendary Harry Hyde (below).

wins in 29 starts, with an amazing 21 top-5 finishes and 24 top-10 finishes. Bill Elliot also had a great year, but it was only good enough for second place. He finished the year with 6 wins, 16 top-5 finshes, and 20 top-10 finshes.

Ford addressed its previous car's shortcomings with a redesign of the Thunderbird. The cars had run well in 1983 through 1986, wining 27 times, but the 1987 Thunderbird was a step up. Under the command of Bill Elliot, this Thunderbird was destined to become the fastest car in the Winston Cup record book.

Elliot won the pole of the Daytona 500 with a speed over 210 miles per hour, but the fastest of Elliot's qualifying runs came in 1987 at Talladega, where he clocked a lap at 212.809 miles per hour. To this day it stands as the fastest lap in the history of the sport.

The reason this record has yet to be surpassed can also be traced to Talladega in 1987. During the race Bobby Allison's Buick ran over some debris, cutting down a tire. As the car began to slide backward, the rear spoiler, which normally keeps the rear of the car glued to the track, caught the

The Politics

Car owner Jack Roush confers with Mike Helton, Senior Vice President and Chief Operating Officer of NASCAR. Teams are in a constant state of lobbying, usually wanting to be allowed a little more air dam or a little less rear spoiler. Most people in racing feel that the squeaky wheel will get the grease.

"That's the politics." These are possibly the three most spoken words in the shops and at the track when discussing controversy. One year the Ford guys are screaming of injustice at Daytona, and the next year it's the Chevy guys going berserk. But before

we get to the rear spoiler and front air dam dimensions and other small concessions given or taken in NASCAR's effort to keep the competition level, we must look at the overall political structure of NASCAR.

The ongoing business of racing is a love-hate relationship between the teams and the NASCAR management. When I say NASCAR management, I mean everyone from the president to the inspectors. NASCAR does not race. It arranges, promotes, manages, enforces, administrates, regulates, and perpetuates, but it does not race. The teams race, and the fans pay to watch the racing.

Often the teams and NASCAR can be antagonists but they both seem to understand that each relies on the other to survive. Without the teams NASCAR has no show, and without NASCAR the teams have no venue. Without NASCAR, the teams would have to unite and have someone to do everything from renting tracks to making rules. Even if they did, they would probably end up just as frustrated.

Keep in mind that the teams ask to run in NASCAR. With the current popularity

action behind the scenes that constantly affects the racing. Tracks are lobbying NASCAR to get race dates and to keep from losing them. Teams are lobbying to get changes to their cars. Any time NASCAR makes a decision, it makes some people extremely happy and some people extremely mad.

Much of the lobbying today centers on aerodynamic advantage. Whichever manufacturer isn't winning will often attribute it to an inherent aerodynamic or downforce disadvantage. As a result of their complaints, the front air dam, rear spoiler, and roof height are often changing, per NASCAR's decisions.

of many drivers, it is possible that they could form their own league and take a good section of the fans, but at what cost? They would find out that the job NASCAR does is extremely difficult and seldom fun. They would find out that NASCAR spends a lot of time dealing with boring administrative detail and dealing with the more than 40 teams, which is like having one ice cream cone to give to 50 kids. But it's worse, because the kids are not able to be interviewed on television and are much less likely to cheat to get the ice cream cone! Chances are after a couple of years, the deserters would be looking around saying, "Whose idea was this, anyway?"

John MacDonald once wrote that the world is not black and white and up and down, the world is gray and sideways. It is this gray

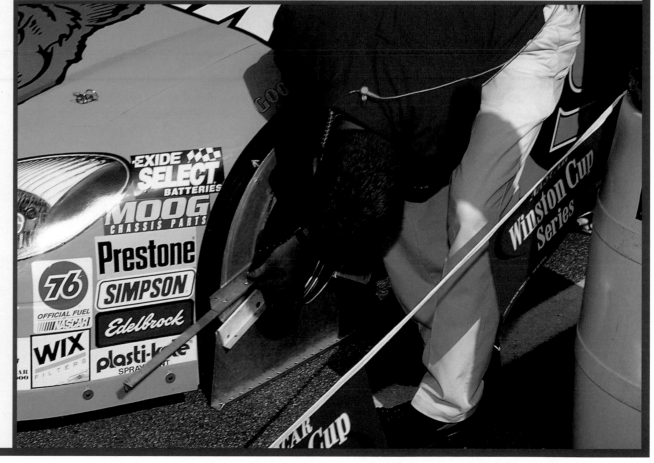

air and lifted the rear of the car upward. The only thing that kept the car out of the stands was the catch fence. Even so, some spectators were injured and the race had to be stopped for almost three hours to help the injured and to fix the fence.

Speed had always been a draw for racing, but if that speed had put a 3,800-pound car into the packed stands, it could have been the end of the sport.

As a result of this accident, the dreaded restrictor plate made its return.

Beginning at the Firecracker 400, the second Daytona race, NASCAR again mandated restrictor plates, just as it had done to lower the big block's power in the late 1960s and early 1970s. This time, however, the plates would only be used at Talladega and Daytona. Because of their length and banking, it was felt that these were the only tracks where speeds were too high. When the teams showed up for the second race at Daytona, the qualifying speed dropped from Elliot's 210.364 from the first race to 198.085. At Talladega the pole speed dropped from 212.809 to 203.827. The plates not only forced the teams to spend a lot more time with their motor programs, it also

Ford won 11 races in the 1987 season. Bill Elliot was most successful with six wins, but newcomer Davey Allison (shown above) was also impressive. Allison ran in only 22 of the season's 29 races, but won twice and had nine top-five finishes. *Don Hunter*

Bill Elliot shook the sport in 1987 with his new Thunderbird. The refined, aerodynamic body, combined with a great engine program, set speed records that will probably never be broken. The fastest record of all came when Elliot ran 212.809 miles per hour in his qualifying run at Talladega. *International Motorsports Hall of Fame*

meant that the aerodynamics of the car would become more and more important. With less power, a car could not force its way through the air. An aerodynamic flaw would be more detrimental to a 500-horsepower car than it would on a 750-horsepower car.

At the end of the season, Chevrolet was still on top, with its Monte Carlo winning a total of 15 races. Pontiac won twice and Buick once to give General Motors a total of 18 victories. The newly redesigned Thunderbird made a good showing for Ford, visiting victory lane 11 times.

1988

In the late 1980s the cars began to undergo another big change. As the cars progressed over the years, the bodies had changed from completely stock to stock with a roll cage. Then the cars became a roll cage with the original body reattached. But in the mid- to late 1980s, the teams quit using most of the factory's sheet metal and fabricated their own. In doing this, teams achieved greater flexibility in creating their car bodies.

The shape of the car is ruled by the templates that NASCAR uses to inspect the car at the track. Each team has an identical set of these templates in its shop. The templates are designed so that when they are placed on the car, officials can determine whether the car's sheet metal is within the tolerance allowed under the rules. The tolerances may be different in different areas. The body may have to be within a quarter-inch of a template in one area, and an eighth-inch in another.

These tolerances leave the teams some room to play with when building the body. By fabricating their own bodies, the teams can refine their cars with small changes. The results of their efforts are then tested both on the track and in the wind tunnel.

Nineteen eighty-eight also saw a perennial NASCAR champion challenged, but it was not a driver, owner, or car that was threatened. It was Goodyear. Goodyear had become the only tire run on the Winston Cup circuit, but in 1988 a small company would offer a challenge. Hoosier had supplied racers in other venues for years, and in 1988 it took a shot at the big time.

It was an interesting battle. When it started, Hoosier had a total of 18 employees and Goodyear had around 350,000. At Richmond, the second race of the year, Neil Bonnett won the first race on Hoosiers, ending a streak of 526 straight races won on Goodyear tires.

By the end of the year, Hoosier had been on nine winning cars out of 29 races. But as the two tire companies fought for supremacy, the safety of the tires was questioned. More and more drivers were being hurt in accidents that were caused by tire failure. The issue ended in 1989 when Hoosier pulled out, primarily due to Goodyear's introduction of a racing radial.

In 1988, all of General Motors' makes enjoyed success on the NASCAR circuit. Chevrolet and Pontiac won eight times each, while Oldsmobile and Buick won two each. Shown are Harry Gant's Chevrolet (top), Neil Bonnet's Pontiac (above), and on next page are Dale Jarrett's Oldsmobile (top) and Ricky Rudd's Buick (lower). *Don Hunter*

Another change in 1988 came at Pocono. Bobby Allison started the race in the 28th position in the Stavola Brothers Buick. On the first lap Allison radioed the crew that he had a tire going down. In the second turn the car spun, backed into the wall, and was then T-boned by Jocko Maggiacomo's Linro Motorsports Chevrolet. Allison was airlifted to a local hospital with serious injuries, especially to his head. It took a long time for Allison to recover, and he would never compete as a driver again. He would, however, return as a car owner.

Another great driver also had a terrible accident in 1988. Richard Petty took a tumbling ride through the tri-oval at Daytona in the first race of the season. When his car finally came to a stop, it was hit hard by Brett Bodine's Ford. Petty somehow escaped serious injury and was soon back racing.

The cars were getting faster and faster, except at Talladega and Daytona, where the restrictor plates got smaller and more restrictive, dropping speeds back to the 190- to 195-mile-per-hour range.

The happiest man at the end of the season was Bill Elliot. He finally got his championship in 1988, and this time he won a close battle. Both Bill Elliot and Rusty Wallace started 29 races, and each won 6. Wallace had more top-5 and top-10 finishes, but Elliot was more consistent and won the championship by a whopping four points. Dale Earnhardt had 3 wins and finished a distant third. As far as the manufacturers went, the wins were more evenly split in 1988. Ford won 9 times, Chevrolet 8, Pontiac 8, and Oldsmobile 2.

1989

Every year drivers come and go, but in 1989 some great ones went. Bobby Allison was gone as a result of injuries suffered in his 1988 crash at Pocono. Benny Parsons, Cale Yarborough, and Buddy Baker all retired in good health. As the season started, there were some mighty big shoes to fill. But other drivers would take their places, graduating to superstar status.

One was Darrell Waltrip, who finally won his Daytona 500 in 1989. In a classic fuel-mileage duel, Waltrip crossed the finish line ahead of teammate Ken Schrader in his Hendrick Motorsports Chevrolet. After the race, an official was asked how much fuel was left in Waltrip's car. The official replied that he did not know exactly, but that he would have drunk it all for five dollars.

While Waltrip finally won the big one, Rusty Wallace finally won the championship. It was another close contest between Dale Earnhardt and Wallace, and it was not decided until Atlanta, the last race of the year. Earnhardt won the Atlanta race and Wallace finished 15th. It was barely enough, as Wallace took the championship trophy by a scant 12 points. He had six wins in 29 starts, while Earnhardt finished the year with five wins.

Thanks to Wallace's Pontiac and Earnhardt's Chevrolet, General Motors ended the decade with its models again dominating the sport. Chevrolet led the GM effort with 13 wins. Eleven of these were split between Earnhardt's Richard Childress Chevrolet and Darrell Waltrip's Hendrick Motorsports Chevrolet, which won 6 times.

After 1989 Chevrolet began phasing out the Monte Carlo from the racing ranks in favor of the Lumina. Pontiac had six wins, all thanks to Rusty Wallace, and Oldsmobile had one, when Harry Gant won at Darlington. Buick also picked up a win from Ricky Rudd in his King Motorsports Buick. Ford was able to rack up eight wins. These were spread between Bill Elliot, who had three wins in his Melling Racing Ford; Davey Allison, who had two in his Robert Yates Ford; Terry Labonte, also with two in his Junior Johnson Ford; and Mark Martin, who scored a single win for Roush Performance.

As the 1980s rolled to a close, the sport seemed to be on autopilot. More money was flowing in from sponsors, fans, and television rights. The competition on the track had always been fierce, but it was becoming a much bigger job to be competitive. Even with the best driver in the world, a team would go nowhere without good chassis builders, engine builders, pit crew, and a crew chief that could put it all together. To succeed at all of these, the first step was to secure a top sponsor.

Top sponsors tended to go to top teams, so fielding a car became a vicious business. Business success was only secured by winning. It became difficult (expensive) to get on top and it was a chore to stay there. In the 1990s it would only become harder. Yearly budget requirements would grow from approximately $2 million to $10 to $12 million by the end of the decade.

Rusty Wallace won the 1989 Winston Cup Championship by 12 points over Dale Earnhardt. Rusty won six times in a Pontiac Grand Prix. *Don Hunter*

The 1989 Daytona race was the last great hurrah for the very successful late-1980s Chevrolet body style. Darrell Waltrip piloted Rick Hendrick's Monte Carlo to a victory in the Daytona 500. *Don Hunter*

133

As the 1990s began, the cars would again change. The sport had grown so popular that the racing budgets were growing by leaps and bounds. These millions in sponsorship money allowed more aftermarket parts to come onto the market. The result was a race car that could be tuned even more finely than before.

Chapter Six

The
1990s

Change was again under way as the sport headed into the 1990s. The cars were becoming more sophisticated and more specialized. More technology, more infrastructure, and more people were involved in the sport. Sponsorship deals were becoming bigger, fueling bigger budgets for the teams, and a greater reliance on science in the search for speed. Men of intelligence and mechanical cunning have always dominated stock car racing. Many of the sport's early competitors, from Junior Johnson to Bobby Allison, had the ability to think through problems and arrive at favorable results, both as drivers and as mechanics.

These men relied on incredibly good reasoning skills, vast hands-on knowledge of cars, and knowledge of the exact results of their tuning when they took the car on the track.

Building a race car and setting it up to perform at its maximum is a very complex matter of physics. Racers in the 1950s and racers in the 1990s battle the same exact physical forces. But in the late 1980s and 1990s, the new technologies that were arriving could help the teams learn much more about what was going on with the car as it sped around the track.

Many of the sport's pioneers had learned on the job and were very much removed from these new technologies. Suddenly, new faces were showing up in the teams. Many of them were young, degreed engineers, and often there was stress between the new science camp and the older, established racers.

When a young engineer, who had very little racing experience, started messing with the race cars, many veterans voiced a negative opinion. The engineers have been ignored, blessed out, and even told to get in the car and drive it themselves. But there is one thing that forgives all sin in the world of racing: winning. When the old veterans began to see the benefit of the new science and the young engineers, they began to warm up to them. Well, maybe they didn't really warm up, but at least they were less nasty.

To be competitive, the team owners found themselves expanding the capabilities of their shop operations. Some were beginning to build their chassis and bodies in-house. They also were stepping up their engine programs.

Suddenly, multiple-car teams were becoming fashionable again. Rick Hendrick started his racing operation in 1984 and since 1986, he has maintained three teams (except in 1991 when he only ran two). Jack Roush came

The cars had changed tremendously since the beginning of the sport, but some things stayed the same. It wasn't David Pearson against Richard Petty any more, but the Wood Brothers and Petty Enterprises still battled in the old 21 and 43. Even as the sport became more and more technical, the old was blended with the new.

to Winston Cup racing in 1988 and expanded to two teams in 1992. He then went to three in 1996, four in 1997, and then to five full-time teams for the 1998–2000 seasons. Roush also had a sixth team that ran a limited schedule. This sixth team has been the stepping stone for both Matt Kenseth and Kurt Busch.

Richard Childress Racing also expanded, adding a second car with driver Neil Bonnett in 1993. After Neil's death, Childress withdrew the car until the 1996 season, when Mike Skinner took over behind the wheel. Robert Yates also added a second car in 1996. The trend was still continuing in the late 1990s as Dale Earnhardt Incorporated, Bill Davis Racing, and Joe Gibbs Racing all added second teams.

There were very sound reasons for these owners wanting to run multiple cars. When they had taken the step to expand their capabilities, they built a lot of shop and bought a lot of equipment.

A team building its own chassis would put up a building and fill it with fixtures, fabrication equipment, and skilled employees. By adding only labor and material, the same facility may be able to produce enough chassis for two or three teams, dramatically lowering the cost per chassis.

The same rule can be applied to everything from the engine shop to the parts area. Joe Gibbs has probably pushed this philosophy further than any owner has. At Joe Gibbs Racing, the cars for both teams are built and prepared under the same roof. Many other multiple-car teams have separate facilities for each car, but the Gibbs way seems to be working. He added a second car in 1999, and within two seasons had won 18 races, a Winston Cup championship, and a Rookie-of-the-Year battle.

On the track, Dale Earnhardt bounced back from his disappointing second place in the 1989 championship race to win it in 1990. Again it was close, as Earnhardt edged out Mark Martin by only 26 points to win his fourth championship, but the victory was not without controversy.

To this day, many believe that a bad decision by NASCAR cost Martin the championship. Martin won the season's second race of the year, at Richmond, after passing Dale Earnhardt and Rusty Wallace.

During postrace inspections, it was discovered that there was an aluminum spacer between the manifold and the carburetor in Martin's car that was 2-1/2 inches tall. By the rules, the spacer could only be a maximum of 2 inches tall. What caused the controversy was that many teams ran a carburetor setup the same height, 2-1/2 inches, as in Martin's car, but in their cars the piece of spacer over the 2-inch limit was welded to the manifold and then glass beaded. In reality, Martin did not gain an advantage, but because his spacer was bolted on, he was penalized.

Martin kept the win but was fined a record $40,000 and 46 points were taken away. Many felt that Martin had received an unduly harsh penalty for what most believe was a very small infraction.

Earnhardt won his championship without setting foot in one of his beloved Monte Carlos. The exclusive Chevrolet ride was now the Lumina. General Motors chose

Dale Earnhardt won the 1990 championship behind the wheel of a Lumina. The venerable Monte Carlo was pulled from the production line for a few years so that the factory could redesign and retool for the new version of the car.
Don Humter

In 1991 Ricky Rudd switched to a Hendrick Chevrolet. Now it was his turn to play runner-up to Dale Earnhardt. *Nigel Kinrade*

the sedan to fill the NASCAR ranks until the new Monte Carlo was ready to go to the public. Yet the Luminas were very successful for Chevrolet. They won a total of 12 races, barely beating out Ford's Thunderbird, which finished with 11 wins. Pontiac added 3 wins, Oldsmobile 2, and Buick 1 to give General Motors a total of 18 wins.

1991

The 1991 season once again started at Daytona. Ernie Irvan had won his first race in 1990, and he backed it up quickly, blowing by Dale Earnhardt with six laps remaining to win the Daytona 500. With the country at war in the Persian Gulf, five cars running the Daytona

500 were painted with U.S. armed forces colors. Alan Kulwicki ran for the U.S. Army, Buddy Baker for the U.S. Marines, Dave Marcis for the U.S. Coast Guard, Mickey Gibbs for the U.S. Air Force, and Greg Sacks for the U.S. Navy.

In 1990 at Michigan International Speedway, future champion Dale Jarrett drove to his first career Winston Cup win. It was the first win for the Wood Brothers team since 1987.

Dale Earnhardt won 4 races en route to the Winston Cup championship, his fifth overall and fourth in six years. Earnhardt's final margin of victory was 195 points over runner-up Ricky Rudd.

Davey Allison and Harry Gant were the series' big winners in 1991, both finishing with 5 wins. Incredibly, Gant won 4 of his 5 in a row. He first won the Southern 500 at Darlington, then at Richmond, Dover, and Martinsville. He would have made it 5 straight, but lost the next race at North Wilkesboro in the final 10 laps. Chevrolet won the race of the manufacturers with 11 wins over Ford's 10. Oldsmobile, Harry Gant's ride, won 5 times, and Pontiac came through with 3 wins.

1992

Nineteen ninety-two marked the end of an era. Big Bill France died in his sleep at the age of 82 in Ormond Beach, Florida. Now the future of the sport was entirely in his son's hands.

Another big change for the 1992 season was when Gary Nelson, a crew chief who often pushed the limits of legality, went from preparing cars to inspecting them for NASCAR. Some said that NASCAR had hired a thief to catch a thief.

Nelson started out with a firm hand. During the first inspection at Daytona, only four cars were approved. The rest had infractions that had to be fixed. Six infractions were

Alan Kulwicki won the 1992 Winston Cup Championship with a small budget and his Ford "Underbird." Alan finished college before he went racing and was one of those who pushed a scientific approach to racing during the late 1980s and early 1990s. *International Motorsports Hall of Fame*

When Joe Gibbs came to Winston Cup racing from the NFL in 1992, some raised an eyebrow. Joe Gibbs Racing has shown, however, that it builds a mean racecar. Gibbs's selections of Dale Jarrett as driver and Jimmy Makar as crew chief proved to be successful. Jarrett would win the Daytona 500 driving a Chevrolet in the team's second year of existence. *Nigel Kinrade*

so severe that fines were levied. Stanley Smith had 8 extra feet of fuel line. Jimmy Spencer had a rear spoiler that lay down below the minimum 35 degrees when the car got up to speed. Harry Gant had copper spacers in the suspension that compressed, allowing the car to run lower to the ground. Some felt that the only reason that Nelson caught them was because he had done it himself and knew where to look. Nevertheless, there was a new sheriff in town, and the teams had to learn to deal with him.

Another landmark for 1992 was the final season for retiring legend Richard Petty. His 1992 "Fan Appreciation Tour" would be his last hurrah. Petty had not had a top-five finish since 1988, and would again go winless in his last season.

A new owner with a proven record as a winner also joined the NASCAR ranks. The only problem was that he had only proven he was good at winning Super Bowls. But it would not take Joe Gibbs long to win in a second major American sport. He hired Dale Jarrett to drive and Jimmy Makar to be crew chief. At the time they had both won races (Jarrett once with the Wood Brothers in 1991, and Makar twice with Rusty Wallace in 1991), but they were still somewhat unproven commodities. That would change.

The 1992 season saw one of the greatest points races ever and an underdog victory that ranks right up there with the U.S. hockey victory over the Russians at the 1980 Olympics.

Entering the last race of the year, a 500-miler at Atlanta, Davey Allison was leading in the points. He was 30 points ahead of Alan Kulwicki and 40 ahead of Bill Elliot. If Allison could finish the race in sixth place or better he would clinch the championship. But Allison lost his chance on lap 253, when he got tangled up in someone else's wreck while running in sixth place, and his day was over. Elliot and Kulwicki battled the rest of the day, both leading as many laps as possible to try to capture the five bonus points given to the driver who leads the most laps.

Elliot won the race but Kulwicki led the most laps, one more than Elliot did. Had Elliot led one more lap, he would have received the 5 bonus points instead of Kulwicki. If that had happened, the points would have been tied and Elliot would have won the championship, as the tie-breaker was based on the driver's number of wins during the season. Elliot won five times in 1992 and Kulwicki only won twice, but Kulwicki won the championship by 10 points, the closest points finish in the history of NASCAR.

Alan Kulwicki was a different breed of racer. He earned an engineering degree from the University of Wisconsin before going racing. When he did go racing, he did it his way. Alan won Rookie-of-the-Year honors in 1986 with only two cars and two full-time pit crewmen. He relied on science, volunteers, and ingenuity.

Even when he won his Winston Cup championship, he did it with one of the smaller budgets on the circuit. At the time, many top teams were working with a budget of around $3 million. But Kulwicki won on a budget that most claim was only $1–$1-1/2 million.

Even though Bill Elliot finished second in the championship, he had an impressive run in 1992. He pulled a "Harry Gant" and won four races in a row at four very difficult, and very different, tracks. He won first at Rockingham, then Richmond, then Atlanta, and capped the run off with a win at Darlington.

Also, an old track got a new face in 1992. Bristol went from an asphalt surface to concrete. Darrell Waltrip became the first to master the new surface and win the race.

continued on page 144

As the great Richard Petty retired, a young kid from the open-wheel ranks started driving the cars with fenders. Within a few years, he would shake up the sport and become a multiple champion. Jeff Gordon entered the 1992 season driving a Monte Carlo for Hendrick Motorsports. In preparation for his Winston Cup career, Gordon drove Bill Davis' Busch series car. *International Motorsports Hall of Fame*

Shops

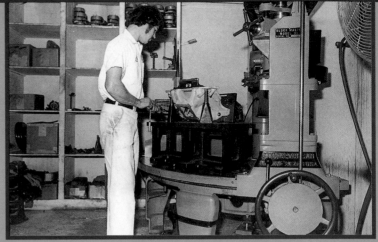

It began with guys tuning up the car in the family garage, a shed, or even the backyard and towing the car to the track. Racing didn't pay much, so the driver usually did everything. By the 1960s and 1970s, the teams were getting a little more room, but the facilities were anything but posh. The teams relied on a couple of cars a year, so they didn't require the room of today's teams.
International Motorsports Hall of Fame

The earliest stock cars were built in basements, garages, and backyards throughout the South. Some cars were prepared in service stations, some in chicken houses. The early race fields were filled with privateers (amateur racers) and many of the first generation of cars were prepared at home. Without big budgets, racers scraped around to find what they needed. The fortunate ones had a large workplace for the cars. The unfortunate worked in sheds, barns, and home garages. It is probable that some of the first "dedicated racing" shops were established because of the latter, after the driver's or owner's wife tired of repeatedly tripping over those six sets of spare springs in the utility room.

At this point in the evolution of the sport, the driver often footed the bills. While some cars might have small sponsors for local events (for example, a restaurant close to the track might work out a one-race deal with a driver), most of the expenses were paid by the driver. And much like today's racing, the prize money was not enough to pay all of the bills. These circumstances dictated the shops be simple and cheap.

The early shops usually housed one car, one toolbox, and whatever spare parts a driver could muster up from the local junkyards. Throughout the 1950s and 1960s, drivers campaigned the same car week in and week out. After a short-track race, the car was retuned to run the super-speedway race the next week. This allowed the drivers to keep the shop simple.

As the sport began to take off in the 1970s, the game changed. There were still guys out there running the same car every week, but the more competitive teams began to learn the advantages of having more than one race car.

As more companies saw the advertising benefit of sponsoring a NASCAR team on a full-season basis, the funds to have more than one car became available. The logic that said two cars were better than one also drove the decision to expand from two cars to three. However, more cars meant more parts, more motors, and more people working on them. And all of this meant more space was needed.

As the sponsorship dollars grew, teams began to set up bigger shops. At first they were in old garages or any other type of building that would suffice. Then teams began to build custom shops. Early shops did not have to house the extreme amount of equipment that they do today. But every year the competition on the track drove an equally furious competition in the shops to engineer better race cars.

Teams began to need space for more machining equipment, diagnostic equipment, and more race cars. Cars began to be built for specific types of tracks. Cars run at short tracks

could not be competitive on the longer tracks. More cars needed more space. Thus the need for a top-notch sponsor became more and more important.

When a company sponsors a team it links its image with the team's. This link is easier to accomplish when the prospective client tours a top-of-the-line facility. During the late 1980s and 1990s this became more of a necessity. Having a full-time sponsor became a "must-have" item. The battle for sponsors often became as competitive as the action on the track. Owners, seeing the importance of these relationships, began to do everything they could to better their chances to land sponsors.

Above: As the sport grew and sponsors became willing to spend a great deal of money to support a winning effort, the shops grew. Teams began to have five or six cars instead of one or two. By the late 1990s, it was common for a top racing effort to have 10 or more cars. Cars were being built a bit differently, depending on the type of track on which they were to race. Short-track cars had large bars in the front end so that the car could survive contact. Road-course cars turned right as well as left, so they were built with a more balanced approach. Superspeedway cars had bodies that were constantly massaged to eliminate drag.

Left and below: The modern shop is not only a spacious place to build cars, it also makes a statement about the team that works there. Owners, seeing the importance of landing a big-time sponsor relationship, do everything they can to better their chances. When a company links up with a race team, their images, to a degree, merge. The image of the team becomes the image of the company. The team with a great shop will run a better chance of landing a top-line sponsor by impressing its representatives with its vast space and equipment.

There is one other reason for the opulence of some of the modern shops. Many team owners and sponsors have been very successful in various business ventures. They have deep pockets and can afford all of the necessities. In fact, they can afford the necessities and then some. And these high-rolling owners also attempt to outdo each other. Polish to these people becomes a point of pride. But it's not foolish pride. The better the impression the shop makes, the better the chance of recruiting sponsors (money) and employees (talent), and the truth of the matter is that money and talent win races.

Continued from page 141

In 1992 Davey Allison's run for the championship in his Ford Thunderbird came up short. Allison had five wins and was becoming a superstar, but he was killed in 1993 in a helicopter crash at Talladega. *Nigel Kinrade*

Opposite: Rusty Wallace did some rompin' and stompin' in his Roger Penske Pontiac in 1993. With its Chevrolet engine, the car won 11 races (10 from Rusty and one more from Kyle Petty) to lead Ford and Chevrolet, who had 10 and nine wins, respectively. *Nigel Kinrade*

On November 15, Richard Petty drove in his last event, the season-ending race at Atlanta. He got caught up in a wreck early in the race, but the crew got the car back on the track so that Petty could take his last checkered flag. Petty finished 35th and climbed out of the car for the last time. Oddly enough, a young future legend named Jeff Gordon got his first taste of Winston Cup racing on the day the King had his last ride.

When the dust finally settled on the 1992 season, Ford led the way with 16 victories. The big winners for the blue oval were Davey Allison and Bill Elliot, who both scored 5 wins. Alan Kulwicki, Mark Martin, and Geoff Bodine each added 2 wins for Ford. Chevrolet finished the year with 8 wins. Darrell Waltrip and Ernie Irvan each won 3 times, and Ricky Rudd and Dale Earnhardt each had a single win. Pontiac had 3 wins—2 from Kyle Petty and 1 from Rusty Wallace—and Harry Gant drove his Oldsmobile to 2 victories.

1993

1993 turned out to be another terribly sad year for the Winston Cup community. A big piece of the sport's future was lost in 1993. Alan Kulwicki was killed in a plane crash flying to the spring race at Bristol. In July, Davey Allison lost his life in a helicopter crash at Talladega. Other drivers stepped up and won races, but one can only imagine what these two uniquely talented drivers could have accomplished had they been able to continue their careers.

But again, the new faces came on strong. Joe Gibbs once again proved his ability to put together a winning team. In the first race of his team's second year in the sport, he accomplished what many have not been able to do in an entire career: He won the Daytona 500. His team had to beat the best in order to do it, as Dale Jarrett edged out Dale Earnhardt on the last lap for the win. Gibbs and Jarrett would not win another race in 1993, but they did finish the year with 13 top-5 finishes, 18 top-10 finishes, and a strong fourth-place finish in the championship. Earnhardt's six wins, combined with 17 top-5 finshes, and 21 top-10 finshes, took him to his sixth championship

Pontiac led the manufacturers in wins with 11. Ford was a close second with 10, and Chevrolet came in a close third with 9. For Pontiac, Rusty Wallace was the big winner. His Penske Pontiac visited the winner's circle 10 times. Kyle Petty won 1 race to give Pontiac their 11 wins. The Ford effort was led by the Jack Roush stable and Mark Martin, who finished the year with 5 wins. Ernie Irvan added 2 more in the Robert Yates ride. He also won a race in 1993 driving

a Chevrolet for Morgan McClure. Davey Allison, Geoff Bodine, and Morgan Shepherd all had single-win seasons in their Fords. Chevrolet's 9 wins came from Dale Earnhardt, Ricky Rudd, Dale Jarrett, and Ernie Irvan.

1994

Another up-and-coming driver found his way to victory lane in 1994. Jeff Gordon, driving a Hendrick Motorsports Chevrolet, scored his first win in the Coca-Cola 600 at Charlotte on May 29. Gordon backed up his first win with a victory at the first Brickyard 400 at the Indianapolis Motor Speedway on August 6. Almost 300,000 spectators showed up to watch the cup drivers compete for the first time at the famed Brickyard. Gordon's team pocketed more than $600,000 for their winning effort. Sterling Marlin also got his first win in 1994, in the biggest race of the year. He piloted the Morgan McClure Chevrolet to win the Daytona 500 in his 279th start.

A new technical innovation made its debut on the Winston Cup circuit in 1994. Roof flaps, developed by team owner Jack Roush, were introduced in an attempt to keep the cars on the track during high-speed spins.

The Winston Cup cars have a good bit of downforce when moving forward at high speed, but when they spin and move backward down the track, the rear spoiler lifts the back of the car. As a result, the cars "take off," much like an airplane. But they can't fly for long, and the resulting crashes are intense. The roof flaps deploy when the air pressure over

the roof changes as the car spins, forcing the car downward. The car may continue to spin, but it is much less likely to get up in the air and flip.

Ford was again the hot brand in 1994, winning 20 of the season's 31 races. Rusty Wallace and Penske Racing, who had switched to Fords, led the way with 8 wins, followed by Ernie Irvan and Geoff Bodine, who had 3 wins each. Dale Earnhardt had the most wins in a Chevrolet (4), followed by Terry Labonte (3), and Jeff Gordon (2). At the end of the year, Chevrolet's total number of wins stood at 11.

For only the second time in the sport's history, Ford and Chevrolet split all of the year's races. Pontiac went from an impressive 11 wins in 1993 to a depressing zero in 1994. With consistent performances and 4 wins, Dale Earnhardt and his Chevrolet won the championship by 444 points over Mark Martin and his Ford. The championship was Earnhardt's seventh, tying him with Richard Petty for most championships won by a driver.

1995

In the mid-1990s the cars reached another new level of refinement. The radial tire offered the cars a much more consistent run on the track, so the geometry of the cars became more important.

Quality control became a big issue for the teams. Teams learned that many "standard" parts that they purchased were not, in fact, identical. If they did not know how the parts were different, they would not know how far their finished product was from the ideal dimensions. The teams demanded that all the parts on the car conform to tighter and tighter tolerances. Every piece was refined. Bolt-on pieces were either bought from high-quality aftermarket manufacturers or were made by the teams.

Even if the complete parts were bought from an outside supplier, the teams still had to check the quality of the part themselves. Most of this quality control work meant measuring the parts. While tape measures and dial calipers were still in the shops, teams began to get better tools with which to measure. One of these tools was the coordinate measuring machine (CMM), which is much more accurate and can measure difficult dimensional relationships much faster than can be done by hand.

The teams were beginning to make more and more of the cars' parts themselves. Teams had used lathes and mills for years, but as the teams grew and staffs became bigger, the shops began to have many more component machining areas, such as Computer Numerically Controlled (CNC) machine centers.

Conventional machining equipment relies on a human operator to control the machine's movements. These machines typically include lathes, mills, drill presses, and

machined. Once the part is secured in the fixture, the operator begins the machining cycle.

At this point the operator can pretty much stand with his hands in his pockets. The machine automatically reads the program, selects the proper tool and makes the desired movements. If the part requires holes of four different sizes, the CNC machine drills one size, changes drill bits, drills the next size, and changes tools again and again (with the operator's hands still in his pockets). After programming the machine and loading the appropriate tools, the operator's main functions are loading and unloading parts, checking the accuracy of the machining after the part is finished, and making sure that the tools in the machine are in proper working order. By saving the program in the CNC machine's computer, the same machining functions can be performed again later with a minimum of setup time.

The primary benefits of CNC equipment are speed, accuracy, and repeatability. Accuracy is better because the machine can place the tool more accurately (and faster) than a human operator. Repeatability is as critical to a Winston Cup team as accuracy. It ensures that

NASCAR inspectors keep a close eye on teams at the track. A mechanic for A.J. Foyt's stock car team is observed here by a NASCAR official as he works under the hood of a Pontiac Grand Prix.

grinders. CNC equipment performs many of the same functions of the conventional equipment, but it offers some big advantages. When operating CNC equipment, the operator programs the desired movements of the machine into its computer. When the programming has been completed, the operator loads the needed machine tools into the machine's "turret." The part that is to be machined is then placed in a fixture that holds the part stable while it is being each part is the same, and that the crew will not have to deal with parts that do not fit. CNC machining changed racing. Everything from cylinder heads to suspension parts began to be created on CNC machines.

As the new season rolled around, an old friend was finally back for the Chevrolet guys. In 1995 the Monte Carlo arrived and made its debut with style. Sterling Marlin piloted his brand-new Morgan McClure Monte Carlo to a

continued on page 151

Diagnostics

One of the biggest elements of success in racing is to understand exactly what every element of the car is doing. It's not enough just to assemble an engine, a chassis, or a body. In order for the team to be competitive, team members must know exactly where they stand with each component of the car before they leave the shop and head to the track.

This is where diagnostic capabilities come into play. The measuring tape is probably the oldest and most common piece of diagnostic equipment in the world. For many years the measuring tape was the primary diagnostic tool the teams had to use, but many new ways to measure have been developed over the last 30 years. Each part on the car is inspected before it is mounted.

Both the size and location of parts can be measured very accurately using coordinate measuring machines. These machines work by linking a measuring probe to a computer. Coordinate measuring machines come in different sizes.

Small machines measure smaller parts. This can be anything from a piston to a control arm. By touching different areas of a part with the probe, the exact dimensions of a single part can be measured to one ten-thousandth of an inch.

A large CMM can be used to measure an entire car. This machine has an articulating arm large enough to reach all around the car. The entire car (body or suspension or both) can be measured much more accurately than with a tape measure and calipers. These machines are very accurate and much faster than old measuring methods.

Other machines measure the performance of various components of the car. One of the oldest is the engine dyno (dynamometer). A dyno measures an engine's torque and horsepower while operating. First, the engine is mounted on the dyno. Connections provide fuel and coolant and siphon away exhaust gases. The dyno also has a brake, which provides

Racer teams have a good bit of freedom in building their cars. The rule book makes some specific requirements but often leaves the team some leeway in how it sets up the cars. One of the more critical areas is the geometry of the suspension. For the finished product to be right, each piece has to be right. Here, a control arm has its dimensions checked with a coordinate measuring machine (CMM). These machines come in a variety of sizes and link a measuring probe to a computer. The result is a quick, easy, and extremely accurate method of measuring. All the operator has to do is touch the part with the probe and the exact point of contact is recorded. As the operator touches more critical measuring points, the computer calculates distances and angles between the selected points. Parts that may take hours to inspect with calipers and gauges can be measured more accurately in minutes using a CMM.

The team will know what each engine is capable of when it gets to the track. Engines are broken in on the dynamometer. The engine will run on this stand just as it runs in the car. All of the engine's support systems are integrated into the dyno system. Coolant, oil, fuel, and air are all piped to the engine to closely resemble the conditions it sees in the car. The dyno is a very important piece of equipment to the engine builders. It enables them to make changes to the engine and immediately find out their effect. Engines can also be run for extended periods to test for longevity and reliability.

resistance to the engine to simulate the drag on an engine as it pulls the race car down the track. Every motor built will go on the dyno. The power output (torque and horsepower) is monitored and recorded at a wide range of rpm. This shows not only how much power is being produced, but also where it is being produced in the power band. The dyno allows engine builders to see the effects of changes that they have made in building an engine, from a different camshaft lift and duration to a new exhaust configuration.

One of the newer engine diagnostic devices used by Winston Cup teams is the Spintron. This machine

The dyno control panel is located in an adjoining room. Here, the operator controls the throttle of the engine with a hand lever. The motor does not just freewheel on the stand. When a motor runs at the track, it has to pull the car down the track. This is also simulated on the dyno. Resistance is applied to the motor by means of a brake, which is incorporated into the dyno. The dyno operator can simulate the different demands placed on the engine by adjusting the amount of resistance.

One of the new additions to the diagnostic arsenal of the teams is the Spintron. An engine is mounted on the Spintron, but it does not run under its own power. Instead, a large electric motor on the Spintron is used to turn the engine to any rpm range the operator desires. While the engine is turning, lasers are used to measure minute movements of the valvetrain. The information is recorded and charted by a computer. One of the first things you notice when observing an engine on the Spintron is the incredible amount of noise an engine makes, even when there is no combustion.

measures minute movements within the valvetrain of the motor as it runs. Instead of making the engine turn with fuel and fire, however, the motor is turned by a large electric motor. This motor turns the engine at any rpm that the engine tester desires. Not only can he select a fixed engine speed, for example, 8,500 rpm, he can also program the Spintron to run a pattern that mimics a particular track.

Different tracks place different demands on an engine. At Talladega, the driver never lets off of the throttle as he goes around the track. But at Martinsville, the driver accelerates at the beginning of the straightaway, decelerates at the end, and may feather the engine through the turn. So when developing an engine for Martinsville, the Spintron can be programmed to accelerate and decelerate the engine along the same time pattern the car takes around the track. In fact, an engine can run an entire simulated race for any track, which will enable the team not only to measure an engine while it is fresh, but also when it is at the end of its projected life.

Knowing the engine's power is important, but it is also important to know how much power is getting to the rear wheels. To gain this information, the team will run the car on the chassis dyno. The car is placed on the chassis dyno so that the rear wheels sit on circular drums that rotate as the tires turn. The car is strapped into place, the engine is started, the car is put into fourth gear, and the throttle is run up to wide open. The power applied to the drums is measured, and the team gets a printout showing exactly how much power is going to the rear wheels.

The aerodynamic efficiency of the completed body can be measured in the wind tunnel. Wind tunnels are just that: a tunnel. At the end of the tunnel a large propeller generates a measured flow of air through the tunnel. In the tunnel, teams are able to see how the air is flowing across the car so they can evaluate where turbulence is generated.

Engines and chassis are not the only parts on the race car that are measured with sophisticated equipment. Some smaller components of the car require their own diagnostic systems. Shock absorbers are a prime example. Shocks have become very important to the handling of the race car. As a result, teams use a "shock dyno" to measure each shock's performance. They measure and record the resistance in both the compression and rebound stroke of the shock absorber.

Even with all of the technology available to Winston Cup teams, some things are still done the old way. Here a crew member "reads" the spark plugs after a short run on the motor.

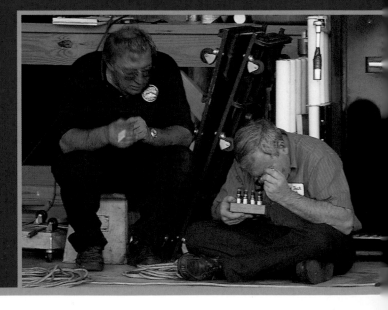

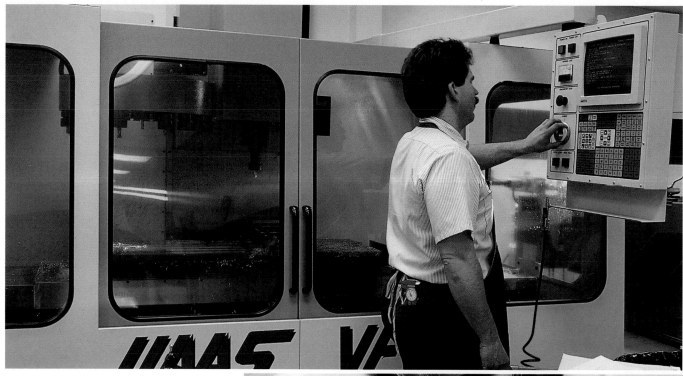

Machining capabilities greatly increase accuracy and repeatability in building race cars. By combining computers and machining equipment, teams can produce high-quality parts, or make modifications to many different parts, knowing that all finished parts were almost exactly alike.

Continued from page 147

win in the Daytona 500. He became one of only three men who have won back-to-back Daytona 500s. The others were Richard Petty, who won the 1973 and 1974 races, and Cale Yarborough, who won in 1983 and 1984.

The Monte Carlo scored another big win when Dale Earnhardt won the second Brickyard 400 at Indianapolis Motor Speedway. The car also turned out to be the ride of the champion. Jeff Gordon, at age 24, became the second-youngest champion in the history of the sport, second only to Bill Rexford, who won the title in 1950 at 23.

Chevrolet dominated the 1995 season with the new Monte Carlo. One of the big factors in the car's success was Hendrick Motorsports, which had become the team to beat. Jeff Gordon led their effort, scoring seven wins. Hendrick teammate Terry Labonte added three more. Dale Earnhardt also had a strong year for Richard Childress racing, ending the year with five wins. Bobby Labonte drove Joe Gibbs Racing to its first multiple-win season, putting

The new Monte Carlo arrived in 1995, and it had a great debut. With a good mix of downforce and drag, the Morgan McClure Monte Carlo won the Daytona 500. In the mid-1990s, Morgan McClure was the team to beat when running a restrictor plate.

their Chevrolet in victory lane three times. Morgan McClure also had a three-win season with Sterling Marlin.

For Ford, the season would yield eight wins. The leader of the pack was Mark Martin, who won four times. Rusty Wallace had two wins and was the only other multirace winner for Ford. Dale Jarrett and Ricky Rudd each scored single wins.

Pontiac had to settle for two wins in 1995. Kyle Petty got one of them, and Bill Davis got his first win as a car owner from Ward Burton, whom he brought on for the last nine races of the season. Randy Lajoie, Jimmy Hensley, and Wally Dallenbach had all driven the Bill Davis before Ward got in the car. Burton scored his win at the last race of the year at Rockingham.

1996

Ford won the big ones in 1996. The season started with Dale Jarrett winning the Daytona 500 driving a Robert Yates Ford. He also won the Brickyard 400 later in the year, becoming the first man to win both races in the same year.

In the mid-1990s, the popularity of NASCAR was soaring. As a result, the retailing of NASCAR-related products was very lucrative. Die-cast cars, T-shirts, hats, and jackets all became hot commodities.

Much of the success of the No. 24 car during the mid-1990s can be credited to Ray Evernham. He not only worked the car himself, but also was also a good manager, expecting and, most often, receiving the best effort from each man on his team. Ray would leave the Hendrick organization at the end of the decade to start his own team, fielding the new Dodge factory effort beginning in 2001.

Dale Jarrett left Joe Gibbs to drive a Robert Yates Ford after Ernie Irvan was injured. In 1996 the team would win both the Daytona 500 and the Brickyard 400. Jarrett would end up with four wins in 1996.

Not only were NASCAR items available in established retail stores, but also from specialty racing stores, television, and the Internet. The first NASCAR Thunder retail store appeared in Georgia. QVC, the television shopping channel, created special NASCAR shows. Daytona USA, an interactive experience for fans (especially kids) that is half-museum and half-arcade, opened on the grounds of Daytona International Speedway on July 5.

NASCAR also went on the World Wide Web on February 14 with the launch of NASCAR.com, which quickly became one of the most popular sites on the Internet.

On the track, Hendrick Motorsports assumed an even more dominant position in the sport. The championship stayed with Hendrick Motorsports, but with Terry Labonte, who had a very consistent year and won the championship by 37 points over teammate Jeff Gordon. Gordon won almost a third of the season's races in his Monte Carlo. Teammate Terry Labonte added 2 more wins to give the Hendrick organization 12.

This strong one-two finish showed that the Hendrick gang was producing cars that were among the best on the circuit. Hendrick had been one of the teams at the forefront of the movement of teams building their own cars. Eddie Dickerson was in charge of building the basic cars for all three Hendrick teams. Once delivered, the individual teams set up the cars independently. The Gordon-Ray Evernham and the Labonte-Gary Dehart driver-crew chief relationships seemed to have the right chemistry.

Chevrolet won bragging rights at the end of the 1996 season, edging out Ford, 17 wins to 13. Again, Gordon led the way. He had scored 2 wins in 1994, 7 in 1995, and 10 in 1996. Terry Labonte, Dale Earnhardt, and Sterling Marlin had 2 wins apiece, and Bobby Labonte had 1 win for Joe Gibbs. Ford's 13 wins came from Rusty Wallace (5 wins), Dale Jarrett (4), Ernie Irvan (2),Rick Rudd (1), and Geoff Bodine (1).

Pontiac won once in 1996, in the hands of Bobby Hamilton.

Nineteen ninety-six would belong to these two Hendrick Motorsports entries. Terry Labonte would win twice, driving consistently throughout the season to win his second Winston Cup Championship in his Monte Carlo. Jeff Gordon had some trouble during the year that hurt his championship run, but he did win 10 races.

Nineteen ninety-seven was the last year for the Thunderbird. Here Bobby Allison Motorsports prepares a Thunderbird to race. Although Allison never won as an owner, his cars were still on the cutting edge of technology. Drivers could feel the difference in handling by just removing one piece of tape from the grille. The stock car was rapidly becoming as cutting edge as any type of race car in the world. The only difference was that Winston Cup cars were on the cutting edge of yesterday's technology.

1997

In 1997 NASCAR was enjoying the spoils of a new track construction boom. Jeff Burton won the first Winston Cup race at Texas Motor Speedway on April 6. Jeff Gordon would win the first race at the California Speedway in Fontana.

But the action on the older tracks was as competitive as ever. To begin the season, Gordon became the youngest driver ever to win the Daytona 500. On May 10, a new record was set at Talladega when 188 laps (500 miles) of racing went by without a caution. Mark Martin ended the race at the head of the pack.

The Ford Thunderbird reached its zenith in 1997, scoring 19 wins among six different drivers. Dale Jarrett led the way with 7 wins. Ernie Irvan added another to give Robert Yates Racing an 8-win season. Mark Martin had 4 wins and Jeff Burton 3 to give Roush Racing a 7-win season. Rick Rudd won twice as an owner–driver, including a win in the Brickyard 400. Rusty Wallace won once, at Richmond in his Penske Ford.

Chevrolet scored 11 wins, all from the Hendrick Motorsports camp. Jeff Gordon again won 10 races and Terry Labonte added another. Gordon's strong performance would win him a second Winston Cup championship.

Pontiac again came through with 2 wins in 1997. Bobby Labonte won 1 race for Joe Gibbs after the team

Ricky Rudd (10) is shown here playing the part of both owner and driver. While owning his own race car offered more control, it also meant more work and more distractions. By 2001 Rudd was driving for Robert Yates, and Brett Bodine was the only driver who owned his own team. Rudd won at least one race in every season from 1983 to 1998.

In 1997 Jeff Gordon again won 10 races in his Monte Carlo, but this time he skipped all the bad luck and won his second Winston Cup Championship.

switched from Chevrolet to Pontiac. Bobby Hamilton was the only other winner for Pontiac.

1998

Another NASCAR legend disappeared at the end of the 1997 season. The Ford Thunderbird was gone, replaced by the Ford Taurus. The Taurus was a more aerodynamic car than the Thunderbird and had much better downforce than the earlier car. The fact that Ford did not offer a two-door model of the car to the public slowed neither NASCAR nor Ford. In fact, NASCAR's efforts to level the playing field among the various manufacturers in the series meant that by

The Taurus debuted in 1998, replacing the Thunderbird. Even though there was no two-door version for street use, NASCAR and Ford worked out a body profile and went racing.

the time NASCAR had balanced the performance of the race cars in the wind tunnel, the finished products had little in common with the factory-body dimensions.

' There are two main areas of aerodynamics that dramatically affect a car's performance: drag and downforce. Drag is simply the resistance the body encounters as it flows through the air. Downforce is the amount of downward pressure that the passing air exhibits on the body.

If you're driving down the interstate and stick your hand out of your car window, you will feel some wind resistance but if you keep your hand level, it will tend to stay in position. But you tilt your hand forward at a 45-degree

angle, the passing air will push your hand downward. You have just dramatically increased the downforce of your hand, but you have also increased its drag.

This explains why new models often don't perform well at Daytona when they are first introduced. They are initially designed to have so much downforce that it slows them on restrictor plate tracks, but this downforce helps at most other tracks.

Downforce is measured independently in both the front and the rear of the car. For the car to handle well, these forces need to be balanced. Current models have about 750 pounds of downforce on the front and back at top speeds.

When the car is running 180 miles per hour, this exerts the same amount of force on the body as putting a 750-pound block of lead on the hood and another one on the trunk when the car is sitting still. The amount of this force increases with speed, so the strain on the suspension changes as the car speeds up or slows down.

NASCAR knows that if one car gains too much of an advantage in aerodynamics, the competition will be hurt.

NASCAR officials primarily use data from a wind tunnel and the race results to even the cars out.

It is common for the officials to take the top finisher from each make to the wind tunnel after a race. There, the amount of drag and downforce can be most accurately measured. They will also watch the race results to make their decision. A good example of the quandary that this can present occurred during the 1997 season. Only one team, Hendrick Motorsports, won in a Chevy. All of the other Chevrolet teams, and there were some good ones, were shut out. So were the Chevrolets at an insurmountable disadvantage? Apparently not, because the car won 11 times, taking victory in a third of the season's races.

At the race where aerodynamics are debated the most, Dale Earnhardt, the all-time victory leader at Daytona, finally won the big one. In one of the most memorable wins in the history of the sport, he won the Daytona 500 in his 20th try.

Mark Martin got the first race win for a Taurus with his victory at Las Vegas in March 1998. The new Taurus

In 1998, Jeff Gordon won his second consecutive championship and his third overall.

had a great first year, scoring 15 wins, but Chevrolet edged the Taurus out with 16 wins. Roush Racing was the hot Ford team with 9 wins, 7 from Mark Martin and 2 more from Jeff Burton. Dale Jarrett also liked his new Taurus, scoring 3 wins.

Chevrolet's season was also a one-team show. Jeff Gordon and his team won a stout 13 races. The only other Chevrolet victories came from the single-win seasons posted by Dale Earnhardt, Terry Labonte, and Bobby Hamilton. Bobby Labonte drove the only winning Pontiac in 1998, visiting victory lane twice. Jeff Gordon's strong season won him his second straight Winston Cup championship.

1999

In 1999 NASCAR celebrated its 50th birthday. The association had grown from the fledgling

The chassis had grown much stronger by the mid-1990s, and it's a good thing.

continued on page 165

Tony Stewart joined Bobby Labonte at Joe Gibbs Racing when Joe expanded to a two-team operation.

Joe Gibbs Racing won the ultimate NASCAR prize in 2000. Bobby Labonte drove his Grand Prix to four wins and the Winston Cup Championship.

Pit Stops

Since early seasons usually consisted of relatively short races, there was no need for a pit crew. As race distances grew, a change of tires and an extra tank of fuel became a necessity. In the 1950s the teams were making pit stops, but not with the ferocity that they do today. Pit crews were most often volunteers and did not have the opportunity to practice their duties extensively. *International Motorsports Hall of Fame*

By the 1960s the pit stops were getting faster but the refinement was not quite there. Note the cowboy boots on the front tire changer. *International Motorsports Hall of Fame*

Over the last few years, pits stops and pit strategy have probably been as responsible for victories as just about any other factor. Drivers who win races seem to be the ones who do a lot of "passing in the pits." Beating competitors in the pits means less work to do on the track. It may take 20 laps on the track to pass another car. A crew can pass that same car in the pits while the driver takes a drink of water.

If two cars are equally matched, they may be able to stay with each other on the track but not be able to pass each other. The pits may be the only place where one can gain an advantage on the other. This is why winning drivers typically compliment their crews when climbing out of the car in victory lane.

An extra second with the car on the jack can mean two or three cars to pass on the track. Even if these cars can be overtaken easily, the driver will use up a little of his tires' traction making each pass. This driver's car

will fade quicker than the other cars that don't have to pass as much.

Performing the required work quickly and correctly is only part of the pit stop. Perhaps just as important, if not more so, is the pit stop strategy. First, the crew chief must communicate with the driver via radio and develop an understanding of how the car is handling. Using only the driver's descriptions, the spotter's observations, and the lap speeds, the crew chief makes a decision as to how the setup will be adjusted. Once the decision is made as to "what" will be adjusted, the crews must decide "how much." If a "loose" car is overadjusted, it may become tight, slowing the car even more. On a race afternoon, a crew chief's train of thought may be something like this:

The car's a little loose with new tires but after about 20 laps, as the fuel load lightens, it tightens up the car and lap times pick up. But it's killing the team on restarts because the car falls back and has to repass the same cars that passed us during those first 20 laps. Is it better to do nothing, and keep relatively the same track position, or make an adjustment to quicken the car on those first 20 laps and risk ruining the good handling characteristics we'll experience later in the run?

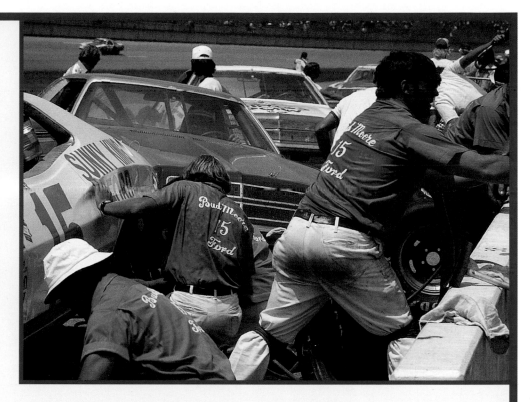

This simple scenario is one of a myriad of situations that a crew chief may encounter during the race. Often the crew chief's problems are much more complicated than this. Not only must he work to make his car faster around the race track, he must also watch the tactical actions of the competition, and be prepared to develop an entirely new plan at a moment's notice in case of a change in the situation. With so many problems to evaluate, sometimes the crew chief's best tool is his ability to listen to and evaluate suggestions from the driver and the other crew members.

The pit equipment has become more sophisticated, just as the

As the competition became closer, the ability to crank off a good pit stop became more important.

With the cars as equal as they are, track position has become more critical. Even if a driver has the fastest car on the track, a bad pit stop can move him from first to twentieth. By the time the driver works his way through all of the traffic (if he can do it without getting caught up in an accident), he will probably have used up his tires and will no longer be the fastest car. Likewise, there is no better way for a driver to pass than in the pits. With a great pit stop a driver can go from fifth to first without using up tires or banging any fenders.

cars have. From lightweight jacks to pit carts with satellite dishes, the variety of tools used in the pits continues to grow. The equipment used in making pit stops can be as important as equipment on the car. More than one race has been lost when a jack or air wrench malfunctioned.

In recent years, with the introduction of speed limits on pit road, the distance lost on the track while pitting is much greater. Teams must carefully choose when to pit in order to minimize the track position lost. Caution flags provide the best time for pitting; however, teams are inevitably forced to pit during green flag racing, or while the racing remains at full speed. For every second a car sits in the pits, it loses distance on the track relative to the other cars.

Jeff Burton drove his Taurus to a win on the new Las Vegas track to get Ford's 500th NASCAR win.

Dale Earnhardt Jr. joined the Winston Cup ranks in 2000 and did so impressively. Earnhardt won two races and also won "The Winston," NASCAR's yearly all-star event. He drove a Monte Carlo built by his dad's shop, Dale Earnhardt, Incorporated.

Continued from page 158

entity of the late 1940s to become one of the world's most powerful and respected major sports powers. It is a shame that Big Bill France was not around to see the 50th year. After studying his past, you've got to feel that the sport had arrived where he had always envisioned it would. The crowds were huge, and the sponsors read like a who's-who of successful American businesses. The teams had reached a new level of polish and the cars still looked kind of stock.

And the media attention was vast. Those greasy, rough-edged racers were written up in everything from *Time* magazine to the *Wall Street Journal*. All the races were televised, as were many of the qualifying sessions. Daily cable television shows featured nothing but Winston Cup material. NASCAR marketed the 50th year with a new logo and a plethora of imaginative advertising, but the racing was all the same—tight, exciting, and unpredictable.

Ford edged out Chevrolet in the win column, 13 to 12. Jeff Burton led the way for Ford with 6 wins and Mark Martin added 2 to give Roush Racing a total of 8 wins. Dale Jarrett scored 4 wins for Ford and Robert Yates, while Rusty Wallace won once to keep Penske Racing in the winner's circle.

Chevrolet's big winner was again Jeff Gordon, who scored 7 victories, including the Daytona 500. Terry Labonte won one race to give Hendrick Motorsports 8 wins. Dale Earnhardt added 3 Chevrolet wins and Joe Nemechek added another with his first career win.

Pontiac had a big year and also had an 8-win team. Bobby Labonte won 5 times and Tony Stewart 3 times, giving Joe Gibbs Racing its 8 wins. Stewart also captured Rookie-of-the-Year honors. John Andretti added another win for Petty Enterprises and Pontiac, bring the manufacturer's total to 9. The 1999 champion was Dale Jarrett, who gave his family its third Winston Cup Championship.

2000

While the racing was spectacular, the 2000 season will long be remembered as a tragic affair. Adam Petty, Kyle Petty's son, was killed in an accident at the New Hampshire International Speedway on May 12. Adam was racing in the Busch series, gearing up to follow his great-grandfather, grandfather, and father as a Winston Cup driver. When the teams returned to New Hampshire, it would get worse. In the same turn, Kenny Irwin lost his life in a crash during practice on July 2 at the wheel of the Robert Yates Ford Taurus.

Another legendary racer announced that he would retire after the 2000 season. Darrell Waltrip would end a 28-year career in which he ran in 780 races, compiled 84 wins, 276 top-5 finishes, and 387 top-10 finishes.

But, as always happens when legends leave the sport, new ones are formed. In his second season on the circuit, Tony Stewart, in a Joe Gibbs Pontiac, followed up his impressive rookie season with 6 wins, 12 top-5 finshes, and 23 top-10 finshes. Another newcomer in 2000 had an old name—Dale Earnhardt Jr. He followed his father and grandfather into NASCAR's elite group of racers. He ran very strong during the first half of the season, scoring points wins at Texas and Richmond. He also won the Winston, NASCAR's all-star race.

As impressive as Earnhardt Jr.'s year was, it wasn't good enough for him to win the Rookie-of-the-Year award. Matt Kenseth, in a Jack Roush Ford, took that honor through more consistent finishes throughout the year. Kenseth had 1 win, a big one, at the Coca-Cola 600 at Charlotte. He also had four top-5 and 11 top-10 finshes.

Defending Winston Cup champion Dale Jarrett began the defense of his crown in excellent form. He dominated at Daytona, winning the Bud shootout and the Daytona 500 (his third). But it was Bobby Labonte who never seemed to get in trouble during 2000, finishing the year with 4 wins, 19 top-5 finishes, 24 top-10 finshes and a Winston Cup championship. Earnhardt again played bridesmaid with another second-place finish in the points. Bobby and Terry Labonte became the first brothers to win Winston Cup championships.

Ford reached a milestone in 2000 when Jeff Burton captured Ford's 500th win at Las Vegas. But the big news at the end of 2000 was that Dodge would be back in 2001. After a long absence from Winston Cup racing, Dodge would reenter competition with the 2001 Dodge Intrepid.

Ray Evernham left Jeff Gordon and Hendrick Motorsports to lead the Dodge effort. To drive his factory-supported, bright-red Intrepids, he chose youth in Casey Atwood, and experience in Bill Elliot. Bill Davis Racing, Petty Enterprises, Ganassi Racing (formerly Sabco), and Melling Racing all made the change to Dodge. All told, it gave Dodge 10 cars shooting to get Mopars into the Daytona 500.

Epilogue

Our look at the future of NASCAR's race cars begins on a sad note. During the 2000 season, each of NASCAR's premier series saw a driver die on the track. In the NASCAR Craftsman truck series, Tony Roper was killed. Adam Petty, driving in the Busch series, was killed at New Hampshire. Kenny Irwin was killed later in the year, also at New Hampshire. These events prompted renewed talk of soft walls. These have been used on some inside walls but the outside walls on all of the tracks remain concrete.

Then Dale Earnhardt was killed in the Daytona 500 at the beginning of the 2001 season. The subject of racing safety became debated by every race fan, race official, and major press entity in the United States.

With all of this attention, surely the biggest changes will occur in the cockpit of the car and the front and rear subframes (especially the front). All of these changes will center on absorbing and dissipating energy. Better seats will help the driver survive the tremendous loads of g-force when crashes occur. The steel tube chassis of the modern car is very stiff. When the car hits a wall or another car, especially head-on, the driver is exposed to a tremendous amount of energy.

To minimize the force on the driver, the car itself will have to absorb or dissipate more of the energy. This can be done by creating zones in the front subframe that are designed to crumple under the pressure of a crash. By crumpling, they absorb energy before the driver has to. Other ideas include energy-absorbing bumpers that transfer the energy of a crash from the front of the car down the sides of the car. Either way, the biggest changes will center on the safety systems of the car.

Developments on the performance side of the car will depend largely on the decisions of NASCAR. The modern Winston Cup cars are very, very similar. Roll cages and front and rear subframes are ruled by tight regulations on material, construction, and geometry, as are body profile and material. Engine power will not increase very much, as they are already performing almost to their maximum. In both of these areas the rules allow little room to experiment. If a team does find a small advantage somewhere, the chances are it will not keep it a secret for long.

So where will the teams get the competitive edge? They will get it from the suspension, where they have concentrated their efforts ever since the engine power leveled out between teams. Suspension geometry will become more and more refined for the track being raced. The components of the suspension will not change much. Coil springs will still be coil springs and sway bars will still be sway bars. It is how they are combined, the sum of all of the pressures and angles that will determine the fastest car. It will reward the hardest worker and the brightest mind— just the way it should be.

Index